Praise for *Unwanted Priest*

"Finely observant, devastatingly honest, and wittily entertaining, Fr Houghton's memoirs—the English manuscript of which had been finished in 1990 but went missing until its rediscovery in 2020—give us a whole new perspective on the sea-change in the Catholic Church before and after the Second Vatican Council. It is all the more poignant because we are right back in the midst of the ecclesiastical 'cancel culture' that he himself lived through, suffered from, and described with incomparable clarity. *Unwanted Priest* is the greatest find in traditionalist literature for decades."—PETER A. KWASNIEWSKI, editor of *From Benedict's Peace to Francis's War*

"Fr Bryan Houghton was a convert Catholic priest whose principles never allowed him to celebrate the post-Conciliar edition of the Mass. At the end of his life he wrote an autobiography in which the reader will meet many key players of twentieth-century Church life in England and abroad. You will agonize with the confessor as he worries about penitents who use the Pill, and how a priest should respond to the liturgical calamities emerging from Rome. You will hear Fr Houghton weighing the difficult choices made by Archbishop Lefebvre and Dom Calvet. It is a book that will encourage priests and people of today to resist tyranny in the difficult times that undoubtedly lie ahead."—FR JOHN HUNWICKE, moderator of "Fr Hunwicke's Mutual Enrichment" blog

"Fr Houghton's touching account of his personal journey in the Faith is accompanied by a spiritual insight of enormous value into the crisis of the modern Church. I recommend this book to everyone."—JOSEPH SHAW, President, International Una Voce Federation, and Chairman, Latin Mass Society of England & Wales

"Divine Providence and the old Mass! Abandonment to the former and adherence to the latter are the *leitmotifs* of the extraordinary life and work of 'the unwanted priest,' Fr Bryan Houghton. From his early Protestant years, through the joys and vicissitudes of his conversion, ordination, parish life, ecclesial controversies, and twenty years of self-imposed exile in France for the sake of the old Mass and the traditional Faith—all recounted with his trademark frankness, humor, wit, and erudition—Fr Houghton estimated that the major events of his life were imposed on him: that he had not had to choose, but only to accept; and consequently, that the principal character of his existence was that ineffable mystery, the grace of God."—ROD PEAD, Editor of *Christian Order*

UNWANTED PRIEST

The Autobiography of a Latin Mass Exile

UNWANTED PRIEST

The Autobiography
of a
Latin Mass Exile

Bryan Houghton

⊕

Edited by
Gerard Deighan

Foreword by
Horatio Conington

CATHOLIC TRADITIONALIST CLASSICS

 Angelico Press

First published in the USA
by Angelico Press 2022
Catholic Traditionalist Classics
© Angelico Press 2022
Foreword © 2022 Horatio Conington
Edited by Gerard Deighan

For information, address:
Angelico Press
169 Monitor St.
Brooklyn, NY 11222
angelicopress.com
info@angelicopress.com

ISBN 978 1 62138 811 1 pb
ISBN 978 1 62138 812 8 cloth
ISBN 978 1 62138 813 5 ebook

Cover design: Michael Schrauzer

CONTENTS

Foreword

Lex Orandi, Lex Credendi

Despite the popularity of science, and the claims and promises made by its adherents, Father Bryan Houghton (1911–1992), whilst taking a keen interest in what science had to offer, none-theless made it very clear that he never sought certainty. After all, what is really worth knowing is beyond our comprehension. The eternal truths transcend human knowledge and understanding. It was faith that he cherished, not certainty, and it was for faith that he prayed. In the words of the original penny catechism, it is through faith, the supernatural gift of God, that we are enabled to believe, without doubting, whatever God has revealed. Father Houghton was a great fan of the penny catechism. A month before he died, the then pope appended his signature to a new catechism, much larger than the one just quoted, and consider-ably more expensive.

Articles 1124 and 1125 of this catechism would have met with Fr Houghton's wholehearted approval. They read as follows:

> The Church's faith precedes the faith of the believer who is invited to adhere to it. When the Church celebrates the sacra-ments, she confesses the faith received from the Apostles— whence the ancient saying: *lex orandi, lex credendi*. The law of prayer is the law of faith: the Church believes as she prays.
>
> For this reason no sacramental rite may be modified or manipulated at the will of the minister or the community. Even the supreme authority in the Church may not change the liturgy arbitrarily, but only in the obedience of faith and with religious respect for the mystery of the liturgy.

Father Houghton placed great store by the maxim *lex orandi, lex credendi*. He simply could not bring himself to celebrate Mass in a form which would belie his faith. But neither could he dis-

1

obey the Church. In his jocular manner, he maintained that it took the changes in the liturgy to make him realise why God had called him to the priesthood—it was so that he could be his own chaplain. Unlike so many laymen, he would not, so long as he was permitted to say it in private, be deprived of the old Mass. Clearly, there are many of us who would argue that God had much more in mind, such was Father Houghton's diligence in the care of souls and the performance of his pastoral duties.

Joseph Jungmann, S.J., observed that there were relatively few people present at Calvary for the crucifixion of Our Lord and Saviour. Even fewer had any notion as to what was really happening. How privileged then are we, he went on to say, who can be present by our attendance at Mass. The Mass and Calvary are one and the same ultimate sacrifice. What we are confronted with is a mystery, beyond normal comprehension, and situated at the very core of our belief. The Mass is extraordinary and should be treated accordingly. If we believe in the Real Presence, should we not then afford it a level of respect at least equal to, but preferably in excess of, that afforded to those of our fellow human beings who enjoy high rank and privilege? After all, we are in the presence of the King of kings, the divine Majesty. Should not our decorum be extraordinary? In action and language the celebration of Mass should be as far removed from the commonplace as it is possible to achieve. Reverence is what is due, and reverence in abundance was what the old Mass afforded—in every gesture, in the sacred texts, in the universal language, in all that the rubrics prescribed, and above all in the wonderful moments of complete silence. It was all of this which Father Houghton so loved and tried so very hard to preserve.

How happy Father Houghton would have been had he lived to see the election of Cardinal Ratzinger to the papacy. Might it be that the cardinal had a hand in including articles 1124 and 1125 in the catechism he was commissioned to compile? It could be argued that their inclusion in the catechism is a surprising one. It is a bit like shutting the stable door after the horse has bolted, but it is a reminder that traditions of hundreds of years' standing should never have been thrown out, and certainly not as a heartless *fait accompli*. Would that the Council Fathers had heeded the axiom *lex orandi, lex credendi*! Would that articles 1124 and 1125 had been on their agenda! Certain it is that we have Pope Benedict to thank for his motu proprio *Summorum Pontificum*, which made the old Mass so much more available. Not even the subsequent motu proprio *Traditionis Custodes* will be able to overcome the momentum of the rediscovery of tradition. It is appropriate that the old Mass was for quite some time referred to as "the extraordinary form," for that is what the act of redemption is: a truly extraordinary act of mercy and forgiveness.

I am sure that were he alive today Father Houghton would have commented on the events which have taken place since his death as evidence of the power of prayer, exhorting us never to give up hope and to put our trust in the workings of divine Providence. It was said of Vatican II that it threw open the doors of the Church to let in the Holy Ghost and that all that followed was the working of the same Holy Ghost. Or was it perhaps that the sudden rush of air extinguished the tongues of fire which so inspired the Apostles? In which case there were still embers glowing beneath the ashes. Father Houghton was just such an ember from which the fire would be rekindled.

In the meantime, in England, one could not help but feel that, in a roundabout way, recusancy had returned. Roundabout, because the old Mass was being stamped out by the Church, not by Protestant reformers. One might go so far as to say that the old Mass was once more driven underground. On many occasions, when he visited England, Father said Mass privately in the old rite behind a curtain in Saint Wilfrid's Chapel in the London Oratory. There were one or two other priests who did likewise. Then, each Sunday, the old Mass was made available in the Little Oratory (strictly speaking, a private chapel). Tongues of fire began to spring up everywhere. Now the London Oratory has more than sufficient priests for the Tridentine Mass to be said daily, and publicly, in the main church. Thus does the Holy Ghost work, but only if there are willing helpers. None was more willing than Father Houghton.

HORATIO CONINGTON

Preface

I never met Father Bryan Houghton, alas, but when I read his autobiography I felt I had. It was at the Abbey of Le Barroux in June of 2009. *Prêtre rejeté*, the French title, was one of the most engaging books I had ever encountered, at once profound and marvellously humorous. It was in French, but a question immediately arose: Did Father Houghton write it in French, or had it been translated from an English original? Of such an original there was no published evidence. I put the question out of my mind, but many years later it returned, for some reason, with great insistency. I donned my sleuth's hat, convinced that the English-speaking world needed ready access to such an important and helpful text, if at all it could be tracked down.

My search led me back to Le Barroux, whose founder, Dom Gérard Calvet, was so highly regarded by Father Houghton. Perhaps Father Edmund, an English member of the community, could provide a clue? Indeed he could, and did—a most fruitful one. He gave me the address of Mr Horatio Conington, who, he said, just might be able to help me. I wrote to Mr Conington, who replied without delay: Yes, he had the original English typescript, from which the French translation had been made.

Shortly afterwards I received the typescript and began the process of editing it for publication. In doing this I have kept as close as possible to Father Houghton's text. For the most part it is a freshly-composed account of his life and thought, though at various points he inserts pieces written on earlier occasions. Some of these are in fact lengthy articles, placed into the narrative at points corresponding to the time of their composition. Their style can differ significantly from that of the rest of the work, and it was tempting to transfer them to an appendix. Ultimately, however, I decided to remain faithful to Father Houghton's eclectic design.

Minor spelling corrections have been made where necessary (e.g., the surname of Fr Stanley Jaki had been misspelled as Jacki).

I am very grateful to Angelico Press for agreeing so readily to publish this book in their Catholic Traditionalist Classics series, alongside their editions of Father Houghton's other and better-known works, *Judith's Marriage* and *Mitre and Crook*. Indeed, in their admiration for the French version, *Prêtre rejeté*, they had commissioned a translator to turn it into English. The discovery of the original made it unnecessary to continue that work.

Father Houghton went to his reward some thirty years ago, but the wisdom so wittily conveyed in his memoirs is as relevant today as ever. As the reader will see, there were two great loves in his life: the immemorial Mass, and the Church of Rome. He remained faithful to both to the very end. It was for him, and continues to be for many, a difficult balancing-act. I believe these pages will help us to accomplish it, inspired by Father Houghton's faith, hope and charity, as by his freedom of spirit and his joy of heart.

GERARD DEIGHAN

1

Childhood to Conversion

I do not propose to write my social autobiography—which might be of interest, as I have met many people far more interesting than I. No, I intend to write my religious autobiography, which, I suppose, can be of little interest to anybody but myself.

In the first place, I am what is normally called "a convert" to Catholicism. But I am quite sure that "conversion" is the wrong word: "vocation" is the right one. God "calls"—and calls constantly from an incredibly early age. The problem is to let oneself be caught by the call. It may take all the ingenuity of an omnipotent God so to arrange our lives that we finally make our assent.

I was born on April 2nd, 1911. I was consequently still only three when the 1914 war broke out. My father was in the regular army and immediately disappeared. Before the war he had been stationed at Greenwich and the family lived in the neighbourhood, at Blackheath.

I scarcely remember my father from early childhood. He certainly had three longish leaves, during one of which I had scarlet fever. But the child-father and father-child instinct is very strong—stronger, perhaps, than the maternal instinct. Anyway, I adored the ground on which my father trod. But I did not really meet him until 1919, when he was stationed in the Isle of Wight for a few months, before being sent off to the Arab insurrection and thence to India. I spent a holiday with him when he was in charge of the citadel in Cairo. And that is practically all I saw of him until he came to die in my house in 1941.

Like all his family, religiously my father was an upright, practising Anglican. That is to say that he went to vespers most Sundays, to matins about once a month, and to Communion twice a

7

year. He subscribed generously to his parish. But he had a Protestant Irish mother, née D'Arcy-Bromlow, who had instilled into him a virulent hatred of Roman Catholicism.

Incidentally, it is difficult to realise in the 1990s how deep-rooted was anti-Catholicism in England up to the 1914 war. The following anecdote must date from 1916. A house opposite us had been taken by a Commander Franks RN and his wife. They had two boys, just like my parents. In 1916 my older brother Geoffrey was aged nine and I was five. The Franks children came between us—about eight and six. I well remember mama telling Geoffrey and me: "You can play with the Franks boys as much as you like and can invite them into the kitchen. But if Mrs Franks invites you into the house, don't go. I should have to call on them—and they are RC." Of course I went into the Franks' house and had a jolly good cream bun—difficult to get in war time. So mama had to call on Mrs Franks and indeed they became good friends—but not socially. I met one of the sons fifty years later, when he was an admiral.

My mother's family was very different from my father's in every respect, including religion. It was dominated by her father, Edward Staples. He was born in the City of London, in Aldwych to be exact, which still had private houses. In some respects he seems to have been the typical agnostic, London liberal of the turn of the century. But his vast experience and brilliant intelligence seem to have veered him towards popery.

I never saw him. He died in India at the age of fifty-eight in 1913. He was a civil engineer of some repute in his day. He could read and write some twenty odd languages, as he refused to sign contracts unless he could understand them in the original and vet the translations. My dear father maintained that his father-in-law was the most brilliant man he had ever met.

Very well, but *obiter dicta* of the great man used to come out during conversation at the dining-room table. I well remember one of these—I must have been over seven, since I was not lunching in the nursery: "I admire the RCs: they swallow the Christian religion, line, hook and sinker. I despise the Protestants: they adulterate the religion by pretending to understand it and by submitting it to the judgment of their own paltry consciences!" I

8

remember the occasion perfectly, after seventy-two years. My only reservation is the word "paltry": another word was used.

I learned much later from my mother that there was a secret tar [scar?] on the family escutcheon. This is the story. In 1913 the great man lay dying in delirious agony. A great friend of the family, who could enter without ringing, a certain Captain Bashford, came to see grandpa. The door to his bedroom was open. He could hear voices. He looked in to make sure that he was disturbing nobody. What did he see? That ghastly Belgian RC priest alone with grandpa. He was obviously trying to get money out of the old man at the hour of death. The gallant captain did immediately what every English gentleman would do: he picked up the priest and chucked him out of the window. Luckily there were rose-bushes below, so the priest got away with a few scratches. Of course the gallant captain saw to it that grandpa had a respectable Anglican funeral. But the Belgian priest wrote to grandma in England to assure her that the Captain had arrived too late and that her husband had already made his submission to Holy Church before he died. Apparently death only occurred a few days after the priest's defenestration, and he was able to bring my grandfather viaticum and anoint him in spite of the gallant captain's vigilance.

Doubtless out of loyalty to her husband and in spite of her agnosticism, my mother took us two boys regularly to church up to the autumn of 1917, when she gave it up. We went to a regency church called St German's on the heath of Blackheath. I loved it: all those pithy sentences like: "if thy eye offend thee, pluck it out" and "the blind man leading the blind." The parables gave me a clear picture and were perfectly comprehensible. The young human being certainly has an innate bias towards religion. I certainly had a very clear idea of God by the age of five or six. He was someone who knew everything, even my most secret thoughts; who could do anything—and in fact did whatever happened. He could punish us for being naughty and reward us for being good. But you could not see him because he had no limit: you can only see the limit, the edges of things. Besides, God was behind everything and everything was in front.

But alas, our visits to St German's petered out. I do not blame my mother. It must have been a tiring job to try and keep a house going in 1917: she had to queue up half the night to get food for us all. But I did think it a bit unfair: we "upstairs" could not go to church, whereas "downstairs" could—nanny and the two servants. They were Irish Catholics provided by my paternal grandmother. They were all under an obligation to go to Mass, whereas we Protestants were under no obligation at all. I asked my mother whether I could go to church with nanny. I remember her hesitating. Doubtless she would have allowed it. But her final verdict was: "No! Your father would never forgive me. You see, nanny is a Roman Catholic."

But divine Providence is not so easily defeated. It must have been in the late autumn of 1917. I had done something terrible: I had stolen some chocolates which mama kept hidden on top of the cupboard in her bedroom. I knew that they were reserved for adults at the end of dinner parties. Anyway, apart from the fact that God had seen me, I realised that I was in for a good thrashing. Where could I hide to cry my eyes out? I went into the drawing-room and hid behind the large sofa. There I knew I should be left alone. There I could die of remorse and starvation.

So intensely was I crying that I never noticed the entrance of Maggie Hogan, the cook, to pull the drawing-room curtains, although she had lit the main gas light before doing so. The first I knew of her was when she crept round the sofa on all fours to console me. "What's the matter, Master Bryan?" she asked me. I explained as best I could that I was in for a good thrashing in this world and for damnation in the next. "Ah sure now, you're not," she said; "you only have to say a Hail Mary and your mother and Jesus will forgive you." So, behind the sofa in the drawing-room, I learned the Hail Mary. Not only did it console me but it worked a little miracle: mama had not counted the number of chocolates there were on the top tray, so she never discovered her loss. Such was my first Hail Mary, my first specifically Catholic prayer. It worked!

But human nature is weak and temptation strong. A couple of months later I climbed up again on top of mama's cupboard. There were no chocolates but delicious after-dinner peppermints. Adam's wretched apple was no temptation in comparison to this. But, after one whole row had gone, I was again overcome by remorse and fear. I ran down to the drawing-room and behind the sofa. I said a thousand Hail Marys and out loud, as children will when sore pushed. It was the same sin a second time. Could God forgive me?

Suddenly I felt conscious that somebody was looking at me from over the sofa. I looked up. It was mama. If only I could die! But she was smiling. "Who taught you that?" she asked; "I bet it's Maggie Hogan." "Yes," I answered. "She's a good girl. And if that is your little chapel, you can go there whenever you want to. And you can tell Maggie to teach you other prayers." If that was not a miracle, I should like to know what is. And dear mama! She, the complete agnostic, was prepared to allow Gnosticism in her little boy. She asked me what I was praying for. It took tremendous courage, but I confessed: "I have stolen some of your peppermints." I expected a good spanking. She hesitated a moment and I could feel her wrath mounting. But she laughed and said: "I suppose it's my fault; I ought to lock them up." My faith in the miraculous power of the Hail Mary increased a hundredfold.

The war ended and papa came home. But he did not return to the home he had left. Four years of enforced separation is a long time for a fairly young married couple. Doubtless my father was dreaming of the hero's return to his wife and children, but my mother had become quite used to living alone and to her independence. Moreover, in 1915 her mother died. This left her a very well-off woman. Had my father been around when his wife came into money, they could have come to some reasonable arrangement. But he was not. My mother had complete control over her own money for more than three years before the war hero returned; and she was certainly not going to let him interfere.

Incidentally, I remember Granny Staples very well indeed, although I was only four when she died. She used to wear enormous, highly perfumed, violet skirts in Shantung silk. When life became intolerable, I could wrap myself round in granny's skirts and cry my eyes out. Mama's skirts were skimpy little things, no use at all. In fact, I had three places of refuge: to lock myself in the lavatory, granny's skirts, and behind the drawing-room sofa.

Anyway, my father and mother made an honourable attempt

to settle down together. My father was stationed in the Isle of Wight. He promptly bought an enormous house, which has since become a girls' school. It had an apartment for his maiden sister, my Aunt Eleanor. Since my mother felt incapable of giving me religious instruction, Aunt Eleanor undertook the task.

Now, Aunt Eleanor was certainly a brilliant teacher. It is over seventy years ago since I received her instructions and I still remember them almost word for word. They consisted in the names and dates of all the mistresses of those horrid Catholic kings of France, Louis XIV and XV, plus a few incomprehensible orgies of RC priests in Naples and rum goings-on among nuns in Canada. It left me with the impression that RCs were certainly very wicked but enjoyed exuberant vitality.

However, the attempt to reunite the family failed. As in the vast British empire there was always a war on somewhere, my father was able to volunteer for the Arab insurrection in 1919. My mother sold the house, put her magnificent furniture into storage, and went off with her two boys to spend the winter at Mentone on the French Riviera.

It was at Mentone that my mother met a perfectly charming old lady by the name of Mrs Roxburgh. She was a widow with two boys, both a bit older than my mother. The elder was married and had just been appointed a judge; he could not come out to visit his mother. The younger was an unmarried schoolmaster who intended to spend Christmas with the old lady. He turned out to be the great J. F. Roxburgh, then at Lancing and later the first headmaster of Stowe.

Now it so happened that my mother rather despised the teaching trade: "people who cannot face life and remain in a classroom until they die," she used to say. But she could not say that of J. F. He was obviously a remarkable man, destined to make a success of whatever he undertook. The result was perfectly clear: Geoffrey, my elder brother, who was rising fourteen, was immediately sent to Lancing in 1920, and I to Stowe some four years later.

But my mother had been brought up in Berlin. Practically all her childhood friends were German. My father and mother frequently spoke German together, which immediately got them classified as spies. The real reason was probably so that we children should not understand. But we children soon got the hang of it! In fact, the easiest way to teach a child a foreign language is to talk it "so that they will not understand." They will learn it in a trice—and without the expense of a teacher.

Anyway, my mother was desperate to get back to Berlin and see with her own eyes how her friends had fared. Geoffrey was at school at Lancing, so he was alright. But what was she to do with her little angel, myself?

She knew that post-war Berlin was practically starving, so she could not bring me with her. She would have to park me somewhere. She found at Roquebrune an RC priest who lodged and instructed ten boys between the ages of eight and eighteen who needed special coaching. Obviously I required special coaching to learn French before I could attend a normal school. I was duly parked on the Abbé Mounier.

There was a bit of trouble about religion. The abbé insisted that I attend Mass every morning as well as a class of catechism. A compromise was reached. I should study French during catechism but should sit at the back of the chapel during Mass, since it would be absurd to hire special personnel to supervise me during Mass. So to Mass I must go.

The Abbé Mounier was perfectly fair about Mass. The chapel was reasonably large. There were brilliant lights on the altar and on the first three rows, where the boys sat. But there were four other rows of pews to the back of the chapel. These were unlit, and I sat right at the back in complete darkness. From my complete darkness I could see the minutest action of the priest perfectly.

The last time I had been to church was years and years ago, when I was a little boy, at St German's at Blackheath. I had loved it: all those parables and pithy saying and the parson telling us all about Jesus. But the Mass was totally different. Fr Mounier turned his back on the boys and never spoke to them. He remained silent most of the time, but when he did speak it was always towards the altar and away from us. We probably were not meant to understand. One of the boys rang a bell from time to time. There was a certain amount of drill towards the start, kneeling, sitting; but after the bells it was all kneeling. At the end,

Fr Mounier gave most of the boys something to eat on the tongue. He himself drank out of a metal cup and shortly after vanished.

It was all most mysterious. The trouble was that I knew practically no French. Fr Mounier and one of the masters knew a bit of English, but I was not going to reveal my ignorance to them. I should have to wait until I knew more French before questioning one of the boys. So there I was, every day, attending the Sacred Mysteries—and it was a total mystery to me. But I imbibed the mystery with all my heart and soul.

The school building was doubtless an old farmhouse. It stood in an olive grove of about two and a half acres with a frontage of some two hundred yards onto the sea. During the summer vacation courses we had classes in the sea, wearing vast sombreros. It was quite idyllic. The staff consisted of the Abbé Mounier and his sister plus one permanent and one part-time "précepteurs"— probably unqualified teachers—from all of whom I received occasional instruction. The boys consisted of a dozen boarders and as many day boys, with whom I was supposed to chatter continuously in order to pick up the language.

Now, the thing that surprised me about the Roquebrune boys was that they took religion seriously. I had two especial friends, both boarders: Bobby L. and Hippolyte de S. They were poles asunder. Bobby, the son of a local doctor, was about eighteen years of age, but totally under-developed. He did not have to shave; he could scarcely read or write. But he was terribly kind and thoughtful about others. He was also immeasurably pious. I regarded him as my protector in case of trouble. Hippolyte was the exact opposite. About fifteen years of age, he was a brilliant bag of nerves. The Abbé Mounier was supposed to calm him down. He used to spend the afternoon up an olive tree singing antiphons to Our Lady in Greek and Latin. The abbé confided to me one day that Hippolyte knew far more Greek than he. Anyway, Hippolyte was very kind to me; and I knew one language he did not: English.

Now it was to Hippolyte that I opened up my problems concerning the Mass. He was about to climb up an olive tree to sing antiphons to Our Lady when I stopped him. It was gross impertinence on my part: I was only nine, whereas he was fifteen.

"I am a Protestant," I said, "and I want you to explain the Mass to me. I attend every day without understanding anything."

"Yes, I have seen you at the back of the chapel. I presumed you were a Jew."

"No, I'm a Protestant. I have attended our own Protestant services and they are very lovely—all about Jesus."

"Yes, 'all about Jesus'—they must be very lovely. But they are not the Mass. The Mass, you see, IS Jesus."

He hesitated a moment. Then: "You see, God became incarnate to redeem us on the Cross. But at the Last Supper he left his body and blood under the appearance of bread and wine as the guarantee of our redemption. That is what the Mass is: the true presence of Jesus Christ, body, blood, soul and divinity, under the appearance of bread and wine. Before such an act there is nothing you can do or say. You can only remain silent. I wish I could join you at the back of the chapel."

Such was approximately Hippolyte's answer. I may have embroidered it a bit over the years, but two ideas remain fundamental: firstly, Protestantism is *about* Jesus, whereas Catholicism *is* Jesus; and, faced with the Redemption, no human activity is possible except silence.

After much wandering around, my mother decided to acquire a pied-à-terre in Paris. At first she shared an elegant, modern flat with her Portuguese friend, Virginia de Castro, in the Avenue de la Motte-Picquet. But after the inevitable row between the two ladies she took a beautiful flat in an old building between Saint-Germain-des-Prés and the Seine. This was as near "home" to me as I ever got.

Obviously I had to leave Roquebrune and go to a proper school in Paris. Actually, my mother found quite a decent boarding school just outside Paris. It was called the École de l'Isle-de-France, and occupied the chateau of Villebon near Palaiseau. It had been rather a grand school before the war and had occupied some splendid chateau in eastern France which was destroyed during the war. It reopened at Villebon, largely, I think, with Protestant money. Anyway, it claimed to be "an English public school" in France. The headmaster was the only English thing about it.

Although, as I have said, I suspect the money was put up by the Huguenots, eighty percent of the boys were Catholic, about fifteen percent non-Catholic, and five percent Jews. There was a permanent Catholic chaplain, one Abbé de Genouillac. He said a Sunday Mass in the parish church next door to the chateau, and a weekday Mass in the chateau chapel, which was rather well attended both by staff and boys.

We Protestants had a service every Sunday evening, alternately Lutheran with Pastor Wagner and Calvinist with Pastor Beugner. It was all rather miserable. Pastor Wagner was a splendid figure of a man, obviously used to addressing several hundred people at a time. Fifteen small boys and three masters with families was an inadequate audience for his magnificent preparations. Pastor Beugner was obviously an intellectual. His real interest lay in the exact meaning of a Greek word in John 22;[1] the rest was immaterial. The proceedings were made more dull and more pathetic by the necessary hymns. Here divine Providence clearly intervened. Among the teachers with their wives and children and among all those boys there was only one who would play the piano to accompany the hymn. This was myself. And this state of affairs lasted for almost three years, from when I arrived, at the age of ten, to my departure at thirteen.

Now, I hated hymns. I do not know why. It is just a fact. When grown-ups talked about "pornography" I thought they were talking about "hymn-singing." Besides, my music teacher, Madame Sauvage, was a devout Catholic and shared my views. She selected three hymns which I could in conscience accompany. When Pastor Wagner expected a rousing hymn, there was not a squeak from lack of accompaniment. The Protestant show was doubtless very good and sincere, but was not exactly terrific.

On the other hand, the school choir from time to time used to put on splendid Masses in the Catholic parish church. I had a

1 There are only twenty-one chapters in the Gospel according to John!

good voice before it broke and I could read music. I was consequently a member of the choir. In the odd three years that I attended the school we supplied several magnificent Masses, usually by French composers. I still have a vivid memory of one: it was Haydn's *Missa Imperialis*.[2] It was not only magnificent but so gay. This is what religion did for you: it gave you a bit of life, of jollity. Forty years later my organist at Bury St Edmunds, Dr Alan Rowe, repeated it for me with organ, full orchestra and professional soloists. It did not deceive me.

Of course I had never seen a High Mass at Roquebrune with priest, deacon, sub-deacon, acolytes, candle-bearers, incense and all the rest. It was perfectly clear that all this pomp and ceremony was not to impress the human assistance but to acknowledge, the least unworthily as possible, the Real Presence of Jesus Christ. It fitted in with what Hippolyte had told me. None of my experiences of Catholicism had corresponded to Aunt Eleanor's instructions. This did not prevent me from believing them—but in a fairly abstract way. Children have several layers of belief; they are, in fact, far more intelligent than grown-ups. But the fact remained: I was a dour Protestant, tied irremediably to Pastors Wagner and Beugner and the three hymns.

The Catholic chaplain, the Abbé de Genouillac, must have been an observant man. I had to bring him one day some papers from my house-master. He took them and then said to me: "I have been observing you for some time. You are really a Catholic. Why don't you become one?" I arose from the chair and faced him with all the dignity of which a twelve-year-old is capable: "Because, Monsieur l'Abbé, I am a Protestant," and I left the room.

Of course both of us were quite right. He was quite right on spiritual grounds. But I was quite right on physical grounds. After all, the world was full of differences. I was English and not French. By the same token, I was Protestant and not Catholic. But I avoided seeing the Abbé de Genouillac again.

But the time had arrived when I had to go to Stowe.

2 This is Haydn's Mass No. 3 in D minor, also known as the "Lord Nelson" Mass and the *Missa in Angustiis*.

Unfortunately, at the precise moment when I should arrive at Stowe, in September 1924 I imagine, my mother and her brother were in China dealing with dues owed by the Chinese government to my late grandfather. My mother had given minute details to her cousin, Lady P., as to how I was to arrive. Unfortunately they all misfired. I arrived at Stowe on my own.

I knew well enough that wine was frightfully expensive in England but that all boys at Stowe were allowed "tuck-boxes." I consequently shipped several crates of decent claret with my luggage. I duly arrived at Finmere Station and took a taxi to Stowe the next morning. We, the taxi driver and myself, discovered the place for tuck-boxes. It was quite enormous and took all the crates of wine.

I then had to face the house-master. I discovered that his name was Acland, and where he lived. But it is a bit frightening for a little boy of thirteen to face for the first time the house-master of a British public school. I thought I had better show some decent sort of kindliness, so I took along a few bottles of my best claret. I knocked on his door and he said "come in."

"I am Bryan Houghton," I said.

"So you're the boy from France. Can you speak English?"

"Yes, I can; but I find difficulty in reading it, and cannot write it."

"Well, we are expecting you. Is your father or mother here?"

"No, my father is in India and my mother is in China. Only I am here. But permit me to present you with a few bottles of the best claret available."

"But you haven't got any more of them?"

"Oh yes! Dozens. You are not depriving me. In fact, I can let you have a couple more."

He was very decent. He explained that in England boys did not drink wine at table, only water. But if I brought all my crates of wine and placed them in the wardrobe at the entrance to his study, I could come every day after lunch and have a glass as was my custom.

Such was my introduction to my native land. What understanding! What liberality! Yes, understanding and liberality are what I most admire among the English gentry. I fear they are on the decline as our great universities become more keen on producing technicians than gentlemen.

Stowe, the seat of the dukes of Buckingham and Chandos, is perhaps the most beautiful place in England. It had become a school about a year before I arrived. The daughter of the last duke, Lady Kinloss, had sold it but continued to live in the neighbouring village of Maids Moreton, where I used to have tea with her a couple of times a term, as she knew my father.

I suppose there were under a hundred boys when I arrived. Most of them were fairly old, sixteen to eighteen, having been superannuated from other schools, principally Eton. There were only three classes: Lower Four B, for those who could not read or write; Lower Four A, for readers and writers; Remove, for the egg-heads who knew algebra and Latin.

I was in Lower Four B because I could not read or write English. It was a tremendous class, full of the most charming and cultured but not very brainy young Englishmen. I well remember the occasion when a master wrote up on the blackboard the three letters C-A-T. He then explained their phonetic value and triumphantly deducted that this spelt "cat." But a hand shot up from the back of the classroom. It was that of the Hon. Alistair B., aged eighteen. "I am perfectly willing to believe you, sir," he said, "but it seems to me so frightfully arbitrary"—as indeed it is. I loved Alistair; I thought him a colossal chap. During the '39–'45 war he became one of our principal spies in Southern Germany but was, I understand, caught and shot early in 1945. It seems fairly clear that one does not have to be frightfully intelligent to have a brilliant career and die a hero's death. What is required is endless common sense plus, of course, endless courage.

But what was the religious atmosphere of Stowe? The school had been founded with money collected by the Reverend Percy Warrington to keep the Anglican Church low. It succeeded beyond his wildest dreams. During my time its religion disappeared down the drain. When I arrived there was no chapel. The gymnasium was used for Sunday worship. It was, of course, obligatory, so we all turned up. The Reverend Mr Habbershon did his best on the stage, the director of music, Dr Brown, strummed on the piano, and we boys all sang ghastly psalms and hymns throughout the ceremony. It was pitiful. It was even worse than Pastors Wagner and Beugner in France.

We also had two classes of "religion" and "ethics" during the week. These were taken by the Reverend Mr Habbershon. Now, I was a very pious boy and had a positive veneration for my pastor. I automatically revered Mr Habbershon. But I could not for the life of me understand what he was getting at. It was all about "pulling one's weight," "playing with a straight bat," "passing the ball," "paying just wages," "treating one's employees as one hoped to be treated oneself." But absolutely nothing to do with the incarnation of God for the redemption of mankind.

As the school grew, we had two more clergymen masters: the deputy head, a Mr Erle, who was said to be high Church; and a rowing blue, Mr Playfair, who was certainly very low.

The time came for my first Holy Communion, at about fifteen in the Church of England. Mr Playfair was meant to be preparing me. I asked him:

"Am I receiving the body of Christ or not?"

"No," he answered, "you are receiving the memorial of his passion."

"Consequently, I cannot commit a sacrilege?"

"No, you cannot."

"Very well, I shall receive your first Holy Communion." I did so.

Now, the Anglican Communion service is so objectively beautiful and pious. It is not and is not intended to be the Mass—the sacrifice of God Incarnate. But as a memorial of the Last Supper it is about perfect. I received Holy Communion in the Anglican Church at least a dozen times at Stowe, and four or five times at the embassy church in Paris. I was also confirmed by the bishop of Buckingham, but this was a pure ceremony, signifying nothing.

What was the religious impact of Stowe during the four very formative years between fourteen and seventeen inclusive? I think I can say that it was directly nil. I do not say that I became anti-Anglican—I was far too English for that. But I certainly became very pro-Catholic. It was during my last year at Stowe that I bought the complete works of De Maistre, of St Francis de Sales, the English texts of St Teresa of Avila, the sermons of

Bossuet and the admirable *Sancta Sophia* of Augustine Baker. I know this to be true because after over sixty years I still have them all.

If my religious education at Stowe left a lot to be desired, my secular education was quite outstanding. I went there unable to read and write English, but after four years, in 1928, I was granted an open exhibition to Christ Church, Oxford. This was highly flattering. I am as grateful to Stowe as I am to Christ Church for their extraordinary endeavour to educate Bryan Houghton.

My best friend at Stowe, one Jimmy Oliver, had preceded me to Christ Church the preceding year. When I arrived I discovered, to my great surprise, that he had become a Catholic. And, moreover, he ascribed his conversion to me! This more than surprised me since I had no intention of becoming a Catholic myself. That the RC Church was historic Christianity none but a fool could deny. But was Christianity true? Indeed was a "true religion" really possible? I was in favour of it politically, culturally, socially, but that did not make it the true religion. I suppose that my position was very much the same as that of Charles Maurras before his conversion. This is curious, because I used to take the *Action Française*[3] at the time, but did not care for Maurras. He seemed to me dogmatic, dull and chauvinistic. I far preferred Léon Daudet, who had life and humour.

Jimmy Oliver told me of how he had broken the news of his conversion to his father, who was a devout, practising, non-conformist. His father had visited him at Oxford and Jimmy began breaking the news in a roundabout way during lunch. His father was growing more and more morose. He suddenly said: "So what Oxford has done for you is that it has made you conform."

"No, Papa, worse than that. I have become an RC."

His father's face lit up.

"Thank God! So you're still a non-conformist!" And all went well.

Jimmy was also very useful in introducing me to the leading Catholics at the time. Ronnie Knox was University chaplain. Mar-

---

3 A French daily newspaper which reflected the ideas of the movement which bore the same name, published from 1908 to 1944.

tin D'Arcy was at Campion Hall. Sligger Urquhart was at Balliol.
All three were very distinguished in their entirely different ways.
I wrote a couple of letters in French for Fr D'Arcy to Henri Brémond, who had badly misquoted his admirable book, *The Nature
of Belief.* Incidentally, I learned later that Brémond's English was
not quite as perfect as he himself imagined it to be. As for Ronnie
Knox, I think the last letter he wrote was to me.

My three years at Oxford were a sort of paradise: an experience of heaven before one had faced the world, instead of the
reward after having faced it. What can be more desirable than to
live in considerable comfort in one of the most beautiful cities of
the world, surrounded by intelligent, civilised and sometimes distinguished people? After all, I met people as diverse as Einstein
and Ghandi with Lord Cherwell; my tutors were Sir Keith Feiling
and Sir John Masterman. I did not have to study; I merely had to
absorb. It was wonderful.

But I fear that I failed to absorb the religion. I was at Christ
Church, the cathedral college. I never went to Communion but
attended matins a few times. The performance was perfect and
the singing magnificent. But is religion no more that singing at a
performance? It did not awaken in me the impulse to adoration,
to surrender, to spiritual obligation, to self-annihilation—to all
those attitudes which religion demands. At the cathedral college
there must have been a number of clerical hangers-on. Not one
ever called on me although I was three years living in college.
This may be an example of the wonderful English lack of "intrusion" into the conscience of another, but a bit of intrusion might
have helped a bright but basically insecure youth.

For two out of three years at Oxford I was president of the
French Club. The French embassy used to send a distinguished
Frenchman once or twice a term to Oxford to deliver a "conference" after coffee one evening. The distinguished Frenchmen
sometimes spent two nights and ate an appropriate number of
meals. I have no doubt but that my long tenure of office was due
primarily to finance and not to my deserts. Of the many distinguished Frenchmen whom I met three stand out particularly:

1. Louis Hourticq, curator of the Louvre. He found everything
wonderful.

2. Darius Milhaud, the composer. He found everything fright-ful.

3. Stanislas Fumet, the author, about whom I propose to write.

George Cattavi Bey, the Egyptian chargé d'affaires in London, was a good friend of mine. He was a bit pompous and serious, but I liked him very much. He wrote me a letter to the effect that the French embassy had told him that they were sending Stanis-las Fumet to Oxford. He proceeded to explain, in his slightly pompous style, that Stanislas was the leader of the Catholic intel-ligentsia in France, a brilliant author and journalist, etc., etc. In fact, I got the impression that Stanislas was a thorough old bore, to be avoided at all costs. However, the French embassy was sending him so I should have to receive him. I arranged some other engagement that evening, so that I could not, unfortu-nately, attend his conference. He turned up in the morning, so I had to invite him and a few members of the committee to lunch.

George's intellectual old bore turned out to be a brilliant young man of about thirty-five. He kept the luncheon party roar-ing with merriment. I had to explain that I could not attend his conference that evening but that I should be round at 10.00 a.m. the following morning to show him round Oxford. We should lunch tête-à-tête before he took the 3.30 p.m. train for London. Stanislas Fumet was to be a big influence in my conversion to Catholicism.

In the meantime something else happened. In those days Christian Dior was a student at the Ecole des Beaux Arts. He used to lunch with us from time to time. One day he mentioned that he was going to Russia with some architect friends of his. There was a bit of trouble about finance. Could my mother help? My mother answered straight away: "I and Bryan will come too, and the money problem will be solved." That was in the early spring of 1932.

Anyway, some fifteen French architects plus Mama and her friend, Suzanne Bertillon, plus Christian Dior and myself all went off to the People's Paradise.

Now it must be remembered that I was by no means funda-mentally anti-communist. One heard absurd stories about condi-tions in Russia, but doubtless the Russians heard equally absurd stories about conditions in England. I took my mother's agnosticism for granted: the ten commandments formed the natural law, which was indeed natural and consequently to be found everywhere. There was no need to bolster it up with religion.

We entered the People's Paradise by sea via Saint Petersburg. Built largely between 1770 and 1830, it had been a very fine city but was a bit decrepit when I saw it. This neither surprised nor worried me. What did annoy me was the intellectual attitude of the guides who were meant to show us round.

For instance, we were given an enthusiastic account of the massacre on the Neva Canal in 1917. There was not a word of apology—"this is the sort of tragedy which happens during revolutions." No, it was a damned good show and ten thousand people were pushed into the canal and drowned. We were, of course, shown the very fine church of St Isaac, turned into an anti-religious museum. There was a great pendulum hanging from the dome. If you pushed it east-west it would gradually turn in a circle—thus proving the inexorability of physical laws. There was a side chapel with a few dozen glass bowls containing preserved male testicles, to show how monks kept their vows of celibacy. There was quite a fine, life-sized icon of Christ crucified, which was just crossed out. And so on.

Later, while in Moscow, I collected some anti-religious posters, which I have still got. Two of them are forceful as pictures but poor as anti-religious propaganda. The first represents the Holy Ghost in the form of a winged money-bag, surmounted by a capitalist top-hat, pouring shekels on some religious dignitaries—a cardinal, an Orthodox metropolitan, a Lutheran, a rabbi, a muezzin, etc. It is well designed and is really rather funny. The second represents the great square in front of Notre-Dame of Paris with the cathedral in the background. To the right stand Cardinal Verdier (Archbishop of Paris in 1932) and Marshal Foch encouraging troops to mow down workers on the left of the picture. Underneath is a quotation from Marx on the Paris Commune of 1871. What is rather naughty about this poster is that in May 1871 the then Archbishop of Paris, Darboy, was shot in prison in cold blood by the Commune of Paris. One must not merely tell a lie but the opposite of the truth; it leaves one's opponents speechless.

I enjoyed my trip to Russia no end. We saw many beautiful things, although we were not allowed to go to Kiev. We sailed down the Volga from Nizhny Novgorod, then over the Darial Pass into Georgia and out through Turkey. But I did not merely enjoy the trip: it also made me think. In the first place, it completely destroyed my mother's agnosticism. The ten commandments were doubtless the natural law, but it required a great deal of supernatural law to keep them operative. The question of cruelty also oppressed me. It was not merely the massacre of the Neva Canal, but we witnessed some direct cruelty as we passed down the great river in the German Republic of the Volga. Yes, cruelty was something which I had never come across before. It came to me as a shock. And it somehow tied up with Christianity, the religion in which God undergoes cruelty—the flagellation, crowning with thorns, crucifixion.

Then there was the trouble of the anti-religious museums. They seemed to me absolute piffle. I could have done better myself! But could I? On the way home I fell ill at Constantinople and had to spend a few days in bed. I whiled away the time in imagining how I should organise an anti-religious museum and what I should exhibit. Obviously one would have a vast whitewashed emporium with crowds of loud-speakers shouting the usual atheist drivel in every language in the world. The pandemonium would be terrific. But what should I exhibit? Atheism is so much the child of the abstract, human intelligence that there is not a single object in God's creation which can represent it. One would have to exhibit "nothing." But nothing does not exit. Of course, every church and cathedral is a religious museum alright—even Saint Isaac's in Saint Petersburg. Of course, one cannot exhibit purely anti-religious stuff. Such was the fruit of my meditation in bed in Constantinople.

I returned to Oxford firmly convinced that I should do something about religion. Religion, moreover, had nothing to do with abstract principles in politics, culture, or sociology. Doubtless all religions had something to say in such matters—notably Christianity—but they were not the criteria for belief. The criterion of belief was quite simply the truth about the person of God.

Now most of my Catholic friends were French and a good

number of these were hard-line Action Française. That is to say that they accepted their religion as the epitome of their political, cultural and ethical thought. Of course, being a Catholic one may accept such views, but one cannot become a Catholic because of them.

This is where Stanislas Fumet comes in. Apart from my childhood friend Jimmy Oliver, he was the first Catholic I had met who was a Catholic for purely religious reasons—nothing to do with politics, culture or sociology. In fact, politically he was a mitigated anarchist. I did not want to become a Catholic for the sake of men but for the sake of God.

I rather forget the dates, but it must have been early in 1933 that my mother left Paris. She took over my father's house in London to look after my elder brother who was about to qualify as a doctor. Incidentally, how grateful I am that my parents never divorced. My father's wife remained my mother. My mother's husband remained my father. How grateful I am and how I admire them for it! They were totally unsuited for each other. But they begat four children, of whom the eldest, my brother, and the youngest, myself, survived.

Very well, I finished Oxford. My tutor, Sir John Masterman, wanted to put me into the diplomatic service. Under divine inspiration I refused. I said I wanted to become a banker. I was duly appointed to a bank in Paris, which was exactly what I wanted, as I could work from my only "home," even if my mother was in England.

Of course I called on the Fumets. To them Christianity was a living proposition, not an abstract principle. I had to spend an hour on my knees in front of the Blessed Sacrament. I had to say my beads—a very rum occupation. Moreover they introduced me to the Comte Biver and his book on the Père Lamy.

I found this book quite remarkable. Père Lamy was not a very gifted man, although he was practical and had a good deal of common sense. But the whole of his life was centred on the divine. Obviously I have no means of telling whether his almost constant visions were objectively real. All I can say is that they corresponded exactly to his real life. Even the most extraordinary of them seemed to fit quite normally into its context. Neither can it be thought that Count Biver had invented anything, since he was about the most prosaic, unimaginative man I have ever met.

Besides, to ascribe all visions to pure imagination does not solve but merely alters the problem. Why should I, when I let my imagination go, usually get dirty thoughts, whereas Père Lamy usually gets a vision of Jesus or his blessed Mother? Visionaries obviously have a saintly imagination, which I lack. Is it acquired by constant practice? In which case they are saints indeed. Or is it a special charisma? In which case they are saints by creation. No, the holiness of the holy and the visions of visionaries deserve rather more attention than is usually given them. As I have already said, I have no means of knowing whether Père Lamy's visions were objectively real or not, but I have every ground for believing that he was a saint—utterly God-centred.

So far I have dealt principally with the vocational side to my conversion: my first Hail Mary behind the drawing-room sofa; the Mass at Roquebrune; the conversion of my best friend; the trip to Russia; the influence of the Fumets and of Père Lamy. But clearly any call requires a response. What was it that I found divinely attractive about the RC religion?

In the first place it was the Mass. And I have a direct experience of this. Before poping I thought it only fair to give Anglicanism, the religion of my baptism, a chance. During the summer and early autumn of 1933 I went regularly to divine worship at the embassy chapel in the Faubourg Saint Honoré. It was beautifully done, as is everything Anglican. Coming home one Sunday after a Communion service I was so wrapped in thought that I missed my bus stop and got carried on to the Odéon. This was only a couple of hundred yards from Saint Sulpice, so I decided to go there. Mass was just about to start. Obviously I had attended both services umpteen times before, but this was the first time that I had attended them on the same day, and one directly after the other. I was also, perhaps, in a particularly receptive mood. Anyway, the difference between the two ceremonies stood out perfectly clearly. The Anglican service was the memorial of the

Passion of Christ in gratitude for our redemption. It was the noblest of human acts, but a human act it remained. The Mass, on the other hand, was a divine act. In his will at the Last Supper Jesus had left his body and blood, the physical evidence of the most inconceivable of crimes—deicide—as the guarantee of salvation of the culprits. The priests were mere executors of this testament. The difference was the one which Hippolyte had pointed out to me at Roquebrune when I was a little boy.

This idea has remained constantly in my mind ever since. The Mass was a liturgy in which God acted, not men. It was largely silent, to allow for adoration of the ineffable presence. What was said aloud was in Latin to prevent the obtrusion of the priest's personality. This basic and early experience must be remembered when the changes in the Mass thirty-five years later are considered.

The second great attraction of the RC religion was the infallible papacy. All other religions seemed based on an immutable sort of totem worship, the vagaries of experts or the illusions of conscience.

Take Bible Protestantism as an example. I tried to read the Bible at twenty-two but found it so immensely boring that I gave it up. I have only completed it (reading Leviticus while asleep) at the age of seventy-five. But anyway, the experts disagree on the simplest passages. Moreover, the written word cannot get up and say: "You are misinterpreting me! What I mean is this." The fact is that no dead letter can be the criterion of belief.

Papal infallibility is a unique claim of the Roman Pontiff—and it is a necessary claim of the True Religion. I can find out what the RC Church teaches by inquiring what the Pope has said on any given subject. This places Roman Catholicism outside and above every other religion. I admit that thanks to the mass media, the Catholic press, a number of bishops, and most priests, it is very difficult to know what the Pope says as I write in 1990. But the mess will clear up in time.

The third attraction of the RC religion was its defence of the moral law. I was a young man. Temptation was coming my way, both sexually and in life generally. I needed a firm guiding hand. The Church gave it as nobody else could.

Lastly, I was overwhelmed by the holiness and discipline in a number of Catholic families which I knew.

This may give you some idea as to why I responded to my vocation.

2

Conversion to Ordination

I was received into the Church on February 21st, 1934 by Monsignor Le Hunsec, Superior of the Holy Ghost Fathers, at their house in the Rue Lhomond in Paris. I was not quite twenty-three years of age. First confession, conditional baptism, Mass and first Holy Communion all take a bit of time. I had to be in the Rue Lhomond, behind the Pantheon, by 6.30 a.m., which meant leaving home (beyond Saint-Germain-des-Prés) shortly after 5.30 a.m., as my mother had taken the car to England and no buses were running at that hour of the morning.

The ceremony went off without a hitch and I was as happy as a lark. Myself and my witnesses, Stanislas and Aniouta Fumet, made our way to the Boulevard Saint Michel to find a café for breakfast, as we were all fasting for Holy Communion. I felt distinctly peckish after getting up so early and my long walk. The great English delicacy of bacon and eggs would not be provided but a decent plate of ham would do. As we entered the café, Aniouta could no longer contain herself. She hugged me and kissed me. "Isn't it wonderful, Bryan?," she said, "now you are a Catholic you will be able to fast!" I thought rapidly: of course, February 21st must be towards the beginning of Lent. My breakfast vanished; just a cup of black coffee and a bit of dry bread.

"Now you are a Catholic you will be able to fast" turned out to be only too true. I seemed to have joined a religion whose primary concern was to keep the faithful's weight down. There was the Eucharistic fast; Lent; fish on Fridays; ember days and vigils popping up unexpectedly throughout the year. It was colossal! And I was to learn that the vast majority of Catholics did stick to the rules. As for the rest, it was a convenient opening for confession. How I admired the sheer discipline of it all!

Immediately after my reception I wrote to tell my mother. I had not warned her before as I was frightened that she might leave my brother in London in order to make a ridiculous row in Paris. She answered in a kind and amusing way to the effect that "I cannot leave your brother without his getting a new girl and I cannot leave you without your getting a new religion." But she told me of my grandfather's conversion on his death-bed. I did not write to tell my father; I thought it would upset him too much. I should tell him later. But this was a great mistake. Of course he learned of my conversion, through my mother's aunt, Great-Aunt Jane—a ridiculous female—which hurt him far more than if I had told him myself.

Of course, in the first ardour of conversion and at the age of twenty-three I immediately thought of the priesthood. But at the same age one also thinks of girls.

There was a French girl, one Francine. She came of a very respectable family. She was eminently eligible. I just ran away from her and let her down. I could have been much kinder.

There was an English girl. She was sexually most attractive. She was, moreover, determined to have me. She came over to Paris every couple of months. One day she turned up for lunch. Louise, my cook, had left lunch on the table as she had to go and look after a sick nephew. I sat down to lunch. Joan turned up stark naked. "My dear Joan," I said, "you may catch cold. In the room through that door you will find my mother's dressing gowns; please put one on." She screamed, disappeared, and I never saw her again.

Then there was an Italian—quite a remarkable young woman, but very dominant. She was a year older than I and probably did not think me mature enough. She eventually married a brilliant Milanese and I am godfather to their eldest son. After sixty years we are still good friends.

Shortly after my conversion I had the visit of a young man whom I had met at Oxford but whom I scarcely knew. I have no idea how he discovered my address and the fact that I had become a Catholic. Like me he was a recent convert. He was accompanying an aged priest who was staying in Paris for a fortnight. Could they both come round for a meal, as he would much like to introduce me to the aged priest? I invited them round the following evening. The aged priest turned out to be Father Francis Burdett, a direct connection of Sir Francis Burdett of the Great Reform Bill and of the Baroness Burdett-Coutts. He was quite certainly the most remarkable man I have ever met. He immediately became my closest friend up to his death in December 1943.

He was himself a convert and became a Jesuit. Mysticism and the mechanism of prayer were his principal interests. He was an authority on Saint John of the Cross and Saint Teresa of Avila. He came to Paris from time to time to visit his intimate friend Henri Brémond, with whose *Métaphysique des saints* and *Philosophie de la prière* he was in complete agreement. His friendship with Brémond got him into trouble with his superiors and he was eventually dismissed from the Society. After being parish priest at Glastonbury he retired to Hanover Square in London as chaplain to the gentry. He immediately exercised considerable influence on me.

Obviously when I had thought of becoming a priest my mind turned to the religious order founded by Père Lamy: the Servants of Jesus and Mary at Ourscamp in the diocese of Beauvais. On the Sunday after my first meeting him, I took Father Burdett to lunch with Count Biver. There were only four of us present: the count and his secretary, Monsieur Charles, Father Burdett and myself. The conversation was most interesting, all about the Père Lamy and his mystical experiences.

However, when we left, Father Burdett advised me strongly against joining Père Lamy's order. I remember perfectly how he summed up the situation: "Count Biver is the last of the commendatory abbots. The wretched prior simply does not count at all. Now, Biver is a simple, devout soul, so the order will vegetate under his rule. But I did not like his secretary at all: a devious character if not downright dishonest. And it is he who will succeed Biver as commendatory abbot. The order will not get off the ground until both abbots are dead—and you may well die before the secretary. Don't touch it with a bargepole. No, you are English and educated. You have a moral obligation to join an

English diocese." He said much more to the same effect and it was very convincing.

I may add that the Abbey of Ourscamp is now flourishing, but both commendatory abbots are long since dead.

However, the priesthood seemed very far away, as I should not undertake it without my mother's consent. I might have to wait until she died.

But suddenly in the autumn of 1934 the whole physical situation altered. My mother had been visiting some friends in Edinburgh. While driving back to London she had a stroke outside Newcastle. Her car went through the hedge and turned over in the field below. Nobody had seen the accident. The farmer, inspecting his property that evening, noticed that somebody had dumped a car in his field. He went to inspect it and found that there was a woman in it, still alive. This was my mother.

My mother was brought to Newcastle Infirmary where she was admirable looked after by a Doctor Hume, professor of medicine at Durham University. He was a charming man and knew my father quite well. His wife was French but, poor dear, was in a Bath chair, crippled by arthritis. I dined with them several times on my trips from Paris and met their three (I think) children: two boys and a girl. One of the boys, a charming lad, is now cardinal archbishop of Westminster.

Yes, this accident completely upset my Paris life. I left the office early on Friday evenings in order to spend Sunday with my mother at Newcastle; and then back to the office for 8.45 on Monday morning. It was not possible. I had to hand in my resignation.

The arrangement in Paris had been that my mother paid the rent, rates, taxes and concierge, and I should pay for the cook, the charwoman and keep myself. But I was earning nothing. My mother was not in a condition to sign cheques for anything, or even to read letters. My home had to be sold. It was a tragic day.

After transporting back to England most of my mother's splendid furniture, after selling the rest, paying wages and seeing to everything, I found, on the eve of my departure, that I lacked the money to buy myself a ticket for London. The telephone had, of course, been cut, so I had to walk round to my most loyal friend, Philippe de Cossé-Brissac, to borrow the odd £10 to get to

England. It is the only time in all my life that I have had to borrow a penny. My gratitude remains enormous.

Doctor Hume made my mother's condition perfectly plain to me. She had had a perfectly normal stroke, but the upset of the car had shifted the position of her heart—and there was nothing one could do about it. My mother would be bedridden for the rest of her days, which might be anything between two months or a year. In the meantime she would suffer from heart attacks every two to three weeks, which would cause her acute pain. But, in view of the fact that she was unlikely to die immediately, he thought she would be far happier in the South of England, where friends could visit her, than in Newcastle, where she knew nobody. He could recommend a good nursing home and an excellent young heart specialist at Cambridge. Would I like him to arrange her transport there? Of course I should, especially as she could not hope to occupy a bed at Newcastle Infirmary for a whole year!

As far as I can remember, my mother arrived in Cambridge just after Christmas in 1934. As Doctor Hume had prophesied, she had a heart attack every two to three weeks. But she only died on July 11th, 1936.

I cannot describe those eighteen months of watching my mother die. Every morning. Every afternoon. Moreover, she was a very dominant character, and the fact that she was totally helpless activated her domination towards me, the only object of her dominion. Had it not been for my morning Mass I should doubtless have caved in—run away. No, I must stick it out!

Then there was the trouble of penury. I lodged in a slum in North Cambridge with a charming working-class young married couple—but childless. I asked them to give me weekly bills which would be duly paid. But the daily expenses were the problem: food, petrol, cigarettes. I finally gave up. I stopped smoking; I parked the car with some friends; I nourished myself out of dustbins. It was not that my mother was unwilling to pay; it was I who simply lacked the nerve to ask a dying woman to cough up.

I left my lodgings early, so as to get to the dustbins before the dustmen called. I soon found the clean and extravagant houses. I collected enough for lunch and for supper. Lunch I had in the botanical gardens where there was good shelter in the event of rain, but of an evening I had to find what shelter I could. This experience has made me a bit hard on beggars. It is not all that difficult to live, even for an amateur like me, but it must be extremely easy for professionals such as they.

It was on the feast of Saint Gregory, March 12th, 1936, that my mother had one of her usual heart attacks. One minute she was screaming with pain, then the next she collapsed. The nurse had been in to give her an injection. There was nothing I could do except to kneel at the bottom of the bed and say a few Hail Marys. I had my eyes shut because my mother was not exactly beautiful when she was screaming. For about a minute I heard nothing. I opened my eyes to see if she were dead. She was looking at me very intently. "Bryan," she said, "you look so beautiful when you pray that I want to become a Catholic. You can fetch a priest tomorrow." Obviously my mother knew nothing about instructions and abjuration and suchlike. She wanted to become a Catholic and was not going to be put off by any half-baked priest.

After Mass the following morning I consulted the admirable parish priest of Cambridge, one Canon Marshall. What reasonably intelligent priest could he send round to receive my mother with a minimum of instruction before she died?

"Divine Providence," he said, "has supplied exactly the man you need. We have a French Canadian priest staying at Cambridge. He is highly intelligent and a bit mad. Your mother speaks French, so there is no problem." Father Louis Brodeur duly turned up. He adored visiting my mother as much as she adored his visits. He received her into the Church and brought her her first and last Holy Communion.

But the real difficulty was getting her confirmed. It was arranged for a day in June 1936. Canon Marshall, Father Brodeur and I were all in my mother's bedroom, expecting the bishop at any moment. Suddenly a telephone call came through from the reception office that a Colonel Houghton and a Major Staples had called to see my mother. They were of course her husband and her brother. Moreover the bishop of Northampton was also wanting to visit her.

Well, well! My father and uncle were shown up the grand staircase and parked in the waiting room. The bishop of Northampton came up the fire-escape and through the window—and disappeared the same way.

I have never seen my mother so gracious and so charming as when she received her husband and her brother immediately after confirmation in the Forbidden Religion. She must have had a good laugh.

She died a fortnight later, on July 11th, 1936. The Requiem was in the RC parish church. It was full. But I imagine that there was only one Catholic present: her son, myself.

My mother left me reasonably well off. I was nothing like as rich as she had been because most of her income came from a life interest in her grandmother's estate, which clearly died with her. But I had independent means. I could do what I liked in life.

Now, the eighteen months of watching my mother die had made me a very disciplined young man. The discipline, added to the vocation of Catholicism, made the priesthood almost inevitable. I wanted to be a priest. This desire had nothing to do with missionary zeal—that I wanted to convert the world. It did not even have anything to do with my personal sanctification. No, I could be just as holy and with less responsibility as a layman. It was the mere fact that divine Providence had so organised my life that I could be a perfectly reasonable priest.

Perhaps I can add here a parenthesis. By watching my mother die I had plenty of time to read. Now, at the start of the century the parish priest of Cambridge had been a Monsignor Scott, who had collected almost everything that the modernists had written, from Lamennais down to Laberthonière. God has not endowed me with particularly opaque stupidity. I could see perfectly well where Lamennais, Loisy, Tyrrell, Laberthonière and company were wrong. I could also see why Von Hügel and Brémond were falsely accused of modernism. Monsignor Scott's library was a great pre-education to my studies in Rome. I knew exactly what modernism was about. It was also a great help when the neo-modernism of Vatican II began to raise its ugly head.

In my opinion, for what it is worth, the two modernisms are quite distinct. The first modernism was entirely composed of gentlemen and aesthetes. They were wrongly engaged in saving the Church through "religious experience"—which led automatically to mysticism. The contemporary modernist is an anti-aesthetic "tough guy" who is engaged in "creating religious experience" by human beings and is opposed to mysticism in any form, apart from charismatism.

I can't imagine Loisy, Laberthonière or Tyrrell approving of Karl Rahner, Hans Küng or Schillebeeckx. As individuals they are chalk to cheese.

In actual fact I think Modernism I is far more dangerous, because more intelligent than Modernism II. The latter, I think, will die of sheer stupidity.

But this is only a parenthesis.

I arranged that I should go in September 1936 to the Beda College in Rome, which had been founded expressly for English-speaking late vocations who had already received "a certain education." Some had in fact received a great deal of education, and most of them even more experience. I suppose that of the forty odd students, some fifteen were late vocation cradle Catholics. The rest were converts like myself, but about a dozen of these had been Anglican clergymen. In view of the number of converts, the curriculum was authoritative and strictly orthodox. Also, the Anglican clergy saw to it that the liturgy was performed precisely according to the rubrics. It gave, in fact, a very good training. I made four personal friends among the students, of whom two became bishops and the other two remained faithful to the old liturgy to their dying day. Incidentally, I was the youngest member of the college.

But the principal influence in Rome was that of Rome itself. In the first place, it was quite clearly the capital of Roman Catholicism. In those days the clergy did not disguise themselves as commercial travellers but wore clerical dress. Wherever you looked you could see crowds of priests, monks, seminarians, nuns, all scurrying around the place. Rome was a clerical city. It was most impressive: these thousands of clergymen and nuns from all over the world, each with exactly the same beliefs, ideals and aspirations—and the vast majority with the same liturgy—all collected in Rome because it was there that resided the Pope, successor of Saint Peter, Vicar of Christ on earth.

Of course, as in most ingenuous human acts, there may have been a bit of pathos in the devotion of all these good and simple people. To them Rome must have appeared, as it appeared to me, the incarnation of the words: "As it was in the beginning, is now, and ever shall be, world without end. Amen!" They were to receive a rude shock some thirty years later.

Then there was their "devotions": the prisons and tombs of Saints Peter and Paul; the Colosseum of the martyrs; down to the catacombs; up to the first church at Santa Maria in Trastevere— and so on. It must have given them, as it did me, sufficient food for piety to last a lifetime. By "piety" I mean a pure emotion— non-intellectual—which puts us in direct contact with the Divine and the Holy. It is generally sneered at by intellectuals. But in my experience only very stupid people believe that we are no more than "rational animals." No, piety is a great gift and a great source of action. I acquired what little I have in Rome.

I spent most of my holidays from the Beda in England, trying to settle my mother's estate. But I also toured southern Italy, Sicily and Malta—where Lord Strickland was particularly kind to me. I also rented a flat at Cortona in southern Tuscany—of which more will be heard later. This I acquired primarily as a bunk-hole from the Beda. But it served a dual purpose. Upon my arrival in Rome I found some very dear Paris friends of my mother's living in frugal poverty off the Knights of Malta. They were Ukrainians. He, Ian Tokarczewsky-Karacziewicz (alias Prince of Takary), had been the last foreign secretary to the independent Ukraine in 1922. I wanted to give them a holiday home which would cost them nothing. Anyway, my flat at Cortona allowed me to explore southern Tuscany, Umbria and northern Latium almost stone by stone.

In fact my three years at the Beda, from September 1936 to September 1939, must have been about the happiest in my life— for the simple reason that I remember practically nothing from them. One remembers disagreeable experiences alright. Well, I had none.

There was so much sabre-rattling in 1939 that I doubted whether there would be a war. Anyway, I had to go back to England in September—some trouble over my mother's will. I passed through Germany. I arrived in England a week before war was declared.

Yes, war was declared. And this among the most civilised people in the world. It was a monument to the fact that human suffering is self-inflicted. When our own pride, avarice, lust, envy, greed and sloth fail to cause us enough suffering, then we must have a jolly good war.

As far as myself was concerned, I had taken my private vows of celibacy and been ordained sub-deacon. I had expected the diaconate in October 1939 and the priesthood at Easter 1940. On the other hand, all my male relatives were either in the army or had volunteered. Should I volunteer too?

I consulted Father Burdett. "No," he said, "don't volunteer. This war is going to be a long one—at least five, possibly ten years. France may collapse but not England. The bishops will have to face a desperate shortage of priests once they have provided the necessary army chaplains and have five or more years of no vocations owing to the war. There will be a shortage of priests but none of soldiers."

I took his advice. I was ordained deacon immediately and priest on March 31st, 1940, by Cardinal Hinsley in the crypt of Westminster Cathedral. I returned to Cambridge, where my mother had died, to say my first Mass. There was nobody present except for my assistant priest, Father Brodeur. How wonderful it was to have nobody there when, for the first time, I consecrated the true presence of Jesus! Nobody to distract me; nobody to interrupt my adoration of the Divine Presence. The intimacy was complete. Of course I have had to say Mass in front of hundreds of people; they tend to distract from the intimacy even when one turns one's back on them.

I had another strong impression from my first Mass and which has never ceased to grow. It was perfectly obvious that Jesus was the celebrant and I was merely a concelebrant. He, not I, was the active partner. When the present fashion of concelebration of Mass by a plethora of priests became the norm I failed to understand it. Their participation could only dim the basic fact that I was concelebrating with Jesus.

3

My First Parish

I was a priest and was due to be appointed.

It so happened that the bishop who had confirmed my mother via the fire escape had died. It was the parish priest of Cambridge, Canon Marshall, who was vicar capitular and ran the diocese. I knew him, of course, extremely well. He called me into his presence. "I know, Bryan," he said, "that the late bishop had promised to send you to the Norfolk-Suffolk border to found a new parish. You are ideal for such a job since you are typically English and you do not need money. The trouble is that I do—or, to be more accurate, the diocese does. The parish priest of Slough has built Catholic schools and lacks the money to pay the interest on the debts. Several alternatives are possible but I am rather loath to take any step which will tie the hands of the future bishop. What I ask of you is this: will you go as curate to Slough and guarantee the interest on the school debt (x hundred pounds) for about a year, i.e., six months before the bishop's appointment and six months for him to decide his action?" I was of course delighted that my few pence should prove immediately useful.

Thus was I appointed to Slough in June 1940. After living with the parish priest for under two months, I moved out in August to the school site in the Farnham Road, opened the school in September and founded a new parish, where I stayed for fourteen years, until September 1954.

Divine Providence certainly interfered in my lodgings in the Farnham Road. Directly opposite the school was a row of cottages, built between 1880 and 1914. The best and most pretentious of these was Lawrence Villa, with double bay windows either side of the entrance. It belonged to a Mrs Sampson. She took me in.

Mrs Sampson was a widow. She herself had worked for some years but her late husband had worked for over forty years with the Stanleys of Derby—a very grand set-up. Mrs Sampson consequently knew exactly how to look after a young gentleman—if I may so describe myself. What really surprised me about her was that she, a practicing Anglican and with a Derby background, should have been one of my first converts. Her only son had married a Catholic and so her grandchild is a Catholic too. It is all very providential.

Anyway, I said Mass on Sundays in the school hall and on weekdays in a cupboard with a window, also in the school.

It was at Slough that I met for the first time any quantity of ordinary English working men. Indeed, on the Trading Estate there was nobody else to meet. Doctors and shopkeepers opened their businesses in the daytime but did not sleep on the premises. The Anglican rector lived at the village of Farnham Royal and there was no resident non-conformist minister. Indeed, at night I was the only educated resident of the North and South Farnham wards of Slough. As such I wielded considerable authority. Even the communists turned up for me to explain certain forms and fill them in. I felt myself very much as must have done a priest during the barbarian invasions at the collapse of the Roman Empire. I was an essential part of the set-up.

Obviously my experience is restricted to the Catholic working man in the 1940s in Slough—and to no one else.

First and foremost the Catholic working man belongs to a depressed class. In Slough the Catholics came in the main from South Wales and County Durham. They were the descendants of "potato-famine Irish" of a hundred years previously who had been imported into the coal mines. Even the coal mines were going, so they arrived in Slough, opened expressly to relieve unemployment in South Wales.

Incidentally I cannot help feeling that the absence of a strong communist vote in England is due to the fact that the hereditarily depressed class is Catholic—and the Catholic is statistically anti-communist. Even the Labour Party has to take account of the

Catholic vote. It would indeed attract a hundred percent Catholic vote if it were a bit less liberal concerning abortion and divorce. The Catholic working man will not vote Conservative because it stands for the Union, but neither will he vote communist because it is anti-religious.

The vast majority of my parishioners were positively loveable. They were loyal to God, to Holy Church and—what was very lucky for me—to their priest. They were also proud of their religion which on the whole they knew very well. In fact it was often about the only thing they did know. As children they had been taught the catechism by heart and had remembered it. It gave them sufficient knowledge to feed their piety. This is the crux of the matter. Nobody expects the laity to be argumentative theologians, but if they lack a modicum of knowledge of their religion they will inevitably fall either into superstition or into infrastition, where superstition means to believe more than the evidence warrants and infrastition to believe less. In those far off days prior to 1963 before bishops and priests could be found to question everything they believed, the laity knew quite a lot about the faith. The focal point of their knowledge, and consequently of their piety, was the Mass.

I did in fact question, very carefully and gently, some simple parishioners concerning what they believed about the Mass. I have obviously forgotten their answers but they ran like this: "Well it's Jesus Christ really present—but dead; the bread and wine separate—what they call a sacrifice. He offers it to God the Father for our sins and to make us holy. We offer it for our dead, ourselves and those we love. We take Holy Communion so that God the Father can see Jesus in us…"

Such an answer seems to me admirable. It implies in fact quite a lot of knowledge. But since then, bishops and priests have been at my parishioners. They no longer feel certain as to what the Mass is about. They fall into infrastition—unbelief—with all its consequences.

I have not mentioned the school. This was obviously the centre of the parish. I had a wonderful head-mistress, one Mrs Galsworthy. She was an educated woman and a lady, which helps a lot. Catechism was the first class each morning and each morning I took a different class. Like that, I could be sure that catechism was duly instructed and that the teachers were orthodox. Incidentally, in my experience the first budding of modernism took place in the teachers' training colleges. I had to dismiss two "supply" teachers who were thoroughly heterodox. I enjoyed trying to teach children, but I doubt if I was any good at it. Anyway, the school grew and grew. I had to sell my mother's diamond solitaire to pay for a massive row of kiddies lavatories.

Of course among the working class one sometimes comes across staggering ignorance and monumental stupidity. Some examples are really rather funny. Take that of Mr N. for instance. He was a first class gardener and what he did not know about pruning fruit trees and roses was not worth knowing. At the age of about fifty-five he decided to become a Catholic. Why, I have no idea. I gave him the usual instructions. He was thrilled. At the end I thought I had better ask him a few questions to make sure that the penny had dropped.

"Now Mr N., you understand that Jesus Christ is both God and man, don't you?"

"Of course, Father. That's it: God and man!"

"Consequently, Jesus Christ is not only God but also…? but also m…? but also ma…?"

"Got me there, Father; got me there!"

"He is also man."

"Of course, man; that's the right word!"

"Now, Mr N., Jesus Christ is not only man but also…? but also G…? but also Go…?"

"Got me there, Father; got me there!"

"He is also God."

"Of course! God—that's the right word!"

Mr N. became an exemplary Catholic. Incidentally, this and many similar examples convince me that the difference between an educated and uneducated man does not reside in their power to understand but in their power to express themselves—above all to themselves, which will give them the power to think. Mr N. understood perfectly that Jesus Christ was God and man but he could not express it to save his life—not even to himself. The penny dropped, but you could not get it back.

The most staggering examples of sheer ignorance which I remember did not come from Slough but from Bury St Edmunds in Suffolk.

I was instructing a couple of perfectly decent girls who wanted to marry Catholics. I had doubtless explained that we believe a great deal more than what falls under our senses, and I added by way of example: "For instance, you believe England is an island although you have never been around it to see." "No it's not," was the concerted reply of both girls. I thought they were being a bit finical and answered: "Well England, Scotland and Wales make an island." "No they don't," came the reply. I was dumbfounded. Where do I go from there? Luckily one of the girls solved the problem: "No! There's Cambridge over there and you don't have to cross any water."

The mind boggles at such ignorance. Here were a couple of girls aged about twenty who have been schooled and are constantly looking at television who firmly believe that England equals the county of West Suffolk and that Cambridgeshire is a foreign country on the same footing as China. I must admit that I admire their local patriotism.

But geography does not seem to be taught in our schools. It was again in Bury St Edmunds. I mentioned to a charming young married woman that I should be unable to give her instructions for a fortnight because I was going to Paris.

"What on earth are you going to do there, Father?," she asked.

"I used to live there before the war and still have many friends."

"Were you a dress-designer before you became a priest?"

It transpired that she thought Paris was a women's fashion shop in London—Paris Modes—and had no idea that it was the capital of France, even if she knew that France existed.

But the strangest converts I received into the Church were certainly Mr and Mrs W. and their four children at Slough. Mr W. had a pony and cart. He was much in demand owing to the shortage of petrol during the war. He had rather a nice council house. His pony lived in the bathroom where the bath served as a manger. Apart from the elder boy, the family did not wash. While visiting my parishioners I used to meet Mr W. and his cart from time to time. One day, he pulled up the pony and said to me:

"Father, myself, my missus and the children all want to become Catholics. How does one do that?" I explained that I should have to come round to give them instructions, as I certainly was not going to have the W. family in my house. So I arranged to call on them each Monday at 9.00 p.m. when they should all be at home. The front door would be left open for me and they would be in the room to the left.

I arrived at 9.00 p.m. on the first Monday. The house appeared to be in total darkness. However, the front door was open. The pony neighed from the bathroom down the corridor, so the W.s were at home. A dim light came from a flickering candle in the room on the left. I looked in but there was nobody there and no furniture. I called out: "Mr W.!" An answer came, apparently from the candle room: "We are all here, Father, come in." I looked into the room again. Strewn around the floor were six large potato sacks. Mr W.'s head was poking out of one of them. "Tell us all about God," he said, and his head disappeared into the potato sack again. I gave each sack a little kick to discover who was inside. I then imparted the eternal truths. Each week saw the same procedure. I received them into Holy Church. They had washed for the occasion. They turned up to Mass from time to time—more often than I had expected. As soon as the war was over they returned to the East End of London whence they had come. I received a couple of letters from them of which the last read: "Dear Father, we are all well except Dad, who's dead."

But did I ever receive educated people into the Church? Were they all staggeringly ignorant or monumentally stupid? When I moved to Bury St Edmunds I received a host of educated people: gentry, magistrates, doctors, dentists, what you will; but in Slough I only remember giving instructions to two.

The first one was an American, Mrs MacT. Apparently the most rapid growing cell in nature is the tip of the onion root. If one can discover how to stop the growth of the tip of the onion root one would have discovered how to stop cancer. Now an English doctor had lots of onion roots growing in the Royal Cancer Hospital in Chelsea. But the said doctor was called up in the R.A.M.C. during the war and somebody had to be found to look after his onion roots. They found a Mrs MacT., a university professor in the U.S.A. whose onions were far less advanced than those at the Royal Cancer Hospital. She sacrificed her own onions in order to look after the English ones. She took lodgings in Slough. She decided to become a Catholic. I instructed her exactly as I had instructed Mr N. I asked her if she believed it.

"Yes," she answered.

"Very well then, I must receive you into the Church."

"But Father," she said, "there is a little difficulty."

"No, no, my dear! Confession solves all difficulties."

"I don't quite think so. You see, I have been married fourteen times, and it would be a pity if I had to divorce my dear old Scotty now that I've settled down."

It was a tough consignment to sort out all her marriages and send the result to the Roman Rota in the middle of war. But I got an answer back: the third marriage was valid. She divorced her "poor old Scotty." She went to a Catholic University in the U.S.A. where she grew solid, Catholic, onion roots.

The second was a brilliant young man, an M.A. Cambridge with some scientific degree. He was excused military service so long as he worked at some scientific project at Slough. He wanted to become a Catholic. I gave him the same instructions I gave to Mr N., the W. family and Mrs MacT. It was a revelation to him. He walked up and down my large study clapping his hand to his forehead: "What vistas you open, Father; what vistas…!" This continued for three months and his enthusiasm never abated. I asked him whether he believed everything I had said. "I believe it implicitly," he replied, "And I hope you will not think that I have wasted your time. It has been among the most wonderful experiences of my life. And from now onwards I shall be a practising Anglican."

Of course ecumenicity did not exist in those far-off days. I should have felt shattered had I not thought the situation immensely funny: three months of Catholic instruction to make a pious Anglican!

However, a few days later was announced his engagement to the only daughter of a multi-millionaire Anglican baronet.

All this chatter about piety, schools and converts has interrupted chronology. I had not been living six months in Lawrence Villa but a new bishop was appointed. He turned out to be a very competent bishop but rather a disagreeable man. I had endowed the parish, so I did not want to move for seven years—the term of my endowment. I asked to see him in order to explain this to him. He answered: "Of course I can give you no guarantee not to move you for seven years. After all, you can give me no guarantee that you won't run off with a woman tomorrow!" This to a newly-ordained convert priest who was trying to be helpful. I left the room, slamming the door behind me. Our relations remained on that sort of footing until his retirement and death. It was a great pity, because he was a competent man.

But the fact remained that I did not wish to leave Slough. Divine Providence arranged that the ideal house came up for sale. Its name was Wyvis Lodge. It was a fairly large house directly opposite the school. It had ten rooms plus offices and an acre of ground. I bought it. The large downstairs drawing room would become the permanent chapel with reservation and for baptisms and confessions. But as far as I was concerned the real importance of the purchase lay in the fact that the bishop could not move me without my consent, since the presbytery and chapel were my private property.

Wyvis Lodge also had, at the end of a long drive, a splendid brick-built coach-house and harness-room plus sheds and pig-sties. As I had about two acres of unused school and church site the other side of the road, I decided to keep goats. These I found to be perfectly charming and most intelligent animals. I cannot understand how our Lord preferred sheep to goats. A farmer up the road had some sheep: immensely stupid animals. Did our Lord prefer the stupid to the intelligent? It is quite possible; but I suspect that when he said goats he was thinking of billies, which are powerful, vicious and smelly brutes. The female however is quite charming and easily housetrained—provided you have no flowers or plants about the place and leave an exit open. I had a young, housetrained animal. She used to follow me upstairs to my study, sniff around the place and lie down on a rug in front of the fire. Then suddenly she would jump up, be down the stairs in a couple of leaps, out of the front door and deliver herself of a few machine-gun pellets or a vast quantity of water. Then, after snatching some sprigs from the drive, in another couple of leaps she would be up the stairs again and in my study.

But the goats made work and took time. I kept three in milk. This supplied ample to provide the canteen for the dances in the school hall to pay for the schools. Goat milk does not taste strong provided you give the animals plenty of wood to eat and no brassica—and cool it off rapidly. I put all my milk in the local dairy bottles and nobody noticed the difference. But of course I had to get up at six o'clock to milk the animals and put them out to graze before Mass at seven-thirty, have breakfast and be in the school by nine o'clock. Monday was reserved for cleaning out the [stalls of the] goats and generally for farming, ending up with instructing the W. family in their potato sacks.

Bright and early one morning a large limousine with a flag on its bonnet drove up to Wyvis Lodge. A smart young officer got out and asked to see me. "He is milking the goats," was the reply, "Go down to the end of the drive, turn right and you'll see him." He really did look grand. The goats all stared at him.

"Are you the Mr Houghton who had a flat in Cortona just before the war?," he asked. "Yes," I replied, "I had a flat and Cortona, but how on earth do you know?"

"Well, you are wanted up at the War Office straight away. I have a car for you at the door."

"Hang it! I've got to milk the goats and put them out."

"You are wanted immediately at the War Office—and service to your country comes before goats."

"Well, has your car sufficient space to put three unmilked goats in it—plus some hay for them to eat?"

"Don't be absurd, Sir," he replied.

"Very well, in this particular case the goats come before my country. Please go back to my house, ring up the War Office and tell them that I am willing to leave Slough at 10.00 a.m. and not a minute sooner."

This he did. Another car was arranged to call for me at 10.00 a.m.

At ten o'clock an indescribable shandrydan rolled up. A major general got out.

"Hallo! You Father Houghton? Splendid! I thought I'd better fetch you myself."

The interview started while we were driving up to Hobart House.

"How on earth did you know that I had a flat at Cortona, since I did not take it in my own name?"

"No, it was in the name of Prince John of Tokary. He was the last foreign minister of the independent Ukraine. One keeps an eye on such fellows, you know."

I should have done much better to take the flat in my own name. The shandrydan duly arrived at Hobart House. Diverse bells were rung. I was shown along with my general into a large room with a big table in the middle. A good dozen people appeared and stood or sat around the table. I sat to the right of my general. Questions were asked by a major at the bottom of the table. Having established that I knew Cortona well, was reasonably observant and had been for walks all over the neighbourhood, the grueling started.

Vast maps were laid on the table.

"Have you walked up that road?"

"Of course!"

"Up to what point is this hill over here visible from the road?"

"All the way up until you reach the summit, when the road turns sharp right and that hill becomes invisible."

"There is a road which turns off to the left here. It continues up the hill, but there is a cross sign at this point. What does that mean? Have you been down there?"

"Yes, I have been down there. All this area is a vast chestnut grove. The cross sign at this point means that the road from the top ends; there is a thirty-foot drop where the road from the bottom takes up. You see, at the chestnut harvest the wagons for the upper grove go along that road, whereas the wagons for the lower groves go around the north of the town and end up immediately below the upper road. But there is no junction between the two."

"But at this point, the hill over there would be quite invisible?"

"Yes."

"Could one put a bridge across from the top end of the chestnut groves to the bottom end?"

"I doubt it. The land falls rapidly away to the valley. Besides, no bridge would be of any use anyway, since you would still have to climb the mountain and be in range of the hill opposite."

"And this path along here?"

"It is visible from the hill about two hundred yards on, just here. After that it becomes very steep and is very narrow." And so on. We covered every inch of ground for about four miles around Cortona.

Thus I left the War Office. I was quite shattered at the competence of the British intelligence service. Not only did they know that I had a flat in Cortona under a different name, but they could lay hands on me. There is superb organization somewhere. Anyway, that was the beginning and the end of my war effort.

The purchase of Wyvis Lodge allowed me to keep more than goats. I could also keep my aging father. It was the only place he could possibly go. My elder brother was in the army and was divorced, so he was no use. Thus, my poor father had to live in a Roman Catholic presbytery.

Almighty God does arrange life most comically. My father, the gallant Colonel G.J. Houghton, D.S.O., was a highly cultured man. He had travelled and fought all over the world. He spoke and wrote half a dozen languages reasonably well. His bedside reading, as I discovered when he came to Wyvis Lodge, was Homer in Greek. But there was one blind spot in all of this culture—and consequently broad-mindedness: his activistic hatred of Roman Catholicism, doubtless instilled into him with the milk of his Irish Protestant mother. That God should give him a son who became a popish priest was bad enough, but that he should be forced to live with him was more than a joke!

At first he managed to walk the half mile to the Anglican church, but he soon gave that up. I asked him if he would like the vicar to call from time to time. "No! It would disgrace me to have to receive him in a Roman priest's house!" A bit later, I said to him: "Papa, you are dying."

"Yes, I know."

"Would you like me to call the vicar?"

"I should not."

"Well, Papa, you ought to say an Our Father or something."

"I shall if you clear out of the room."

Yes, even the Our Father would be sullied by the presence of a popish priest!

He died. The Battle of Britain had begun, and things were a bit disorganised. He was buried in the Anglican cemetery at Farnham Royal church. No representative from the army or his regiment was able to be present. But the church was full of pious Roman Catholics who had come to pay their respects to the father of their parish priest. There was only one Protestant present to answer the vicar, my brother. Thus, my mother was buried a Catholic with only one Catholic present, myself; my father was buried a Protestant with only one Protestant present, my brother. And then you get people who do not believe in divine Providence! Or, if they do, they deny God a sense of humour. I admit that the Redemption is a very serious matter, but the Creation and divine Providence are pure jokes!

As I have said, Wyvis Lodge was a large house. I could not only keep goats and lodge my father but could also house a curate. I suspect with hindsight that the bishop was having his own back on me: if Houghton prevents me from moving him he can d--n well have a curate!

On the Continent the parish priest lives separately from his curate or curates. In England this is not so. One is "married" to one's curate. He is there at breakfast, lunch, tea and supper. This can be a bit of a trial. But on the whole I think the trial is worth it. Most priests must at least acquire the virtue of patience.

I had three curates at Slough, one after the other. The second one was superb. He was Manchester Irish. Thanks to his Irishness he got on perfectly with my father. Then he was short and round. One of the curate's duties was to bring the goats in of an evening. Of course, half a dozen goats pulled Father Paddy over in a trice. They scampered home with Paddy holding on like grim death, but bouncing on his tummy with his little legs beating in the air.

I witnessed the operation when I returned early one day and

went to the lavatory, which overlooked the drive to the goat sheds. It was terrific. I feel permanently indebted to Father Paddy Oates. May his name be immortalized.

I only have one slight criticism of Father Oates. Being myself a convert, I felt diffident of transferring a convert mentality to my instructees. I consequently asked him to instruct the majority of converts. But one day a reasonably cultured convert asked to see me. He said: "I have nothing against Father Oates; I think him a very good man. But he does not answer my questions. He invariably gives me the answer to a question which I have not asked." I could well believe him. It takes considerable patience to listen to a question, considerable understanding to grasp it and considerable competence to give a reply. So I took over the man from Paddy, to whom I gave some excuse. But the problem exists. I have a horrible feeling that a great many present-day bishops are totally blind to the problems which they have to face. They are constantly giving answers to questions which nobody except their immediate entourage is asking.

I mention all this because it explains how I became interested in the education of priests. They must be taught to see the question before they came out with the wrong answer.

4

The Higher
Studies Conference

In those distant days there was an institution known as the
Higher Studies Conference. It was composed of all the professors
who were engaged in training priests in England, be they secular
or regular. A few interested non-professors were allowed to
attend. It met during Easter week, from Monday evening until
Saturday morning. Two papers of one-and-a-half hours each
were read morning and late afternoon, followed by discussion.
The object of the exercise was to keep the professorial staff up to
date and to ensure some sort of homogeneity in what they
taught. The Conference was run by a secretary, elected for five
years, but not renewable, helped by a committee elected for
three years, but renewable. About eighty to a hundred priests
turned up each year, the majority seculars, but the intelligentsia
was largely Benedictine and Jesuit. The Conference was recognised by Rome, and one was allowed to discuss "quod tuto non
doceri potest"—what was not allowed to be taught.

It so happened that during the war, 1940 to 1945, the secretary
was the provost of my diocese, one Charles Davidson, than whom
it would be impossible to meet a more charming or cultured man.
I asked to be invited as a university graduate who was interested
in the education of the secular clergy. It seemed to me that the
seminary system was quite inadequate. One became a priest by
attending lectures and passing oral examinations, but one scarcely
ever had to put pen to paper. At least a full-dress essay of twenty-
five pages should be required twice a term so as to force the habit
of writing, force examining the questions to be answered, force
organisation of the material, force a modicum of private study,

etc. Here you have a batch of particularly willing, "vocational" students, who are practically deprived of studying at all!

"The easiest way to invite you," answered Provost Davidson, "would be to ask you to write a paper on 'The Final Product: the Parish Priest.' As PP of Slough Trading Estate nobody would dare contradict you." This was done at Easter 1945.

I wish at this point to make a parenthesis. Since 1964/1969 one has reason to be a little shocked at the subservience of the clergy to the fantastic demands put upon them. They all said the old Mass according to the rubrics. They have become impresarios exhibiting the new liturgy. This could not have happened had they been more solidly educated. But their seminary course was a series of lectures, and they are naturally willing to follow the lectures of their bishops. Had they studied the problems involved they might have acquired a few convictions—and consequently a bit of independence.

Obviously, I have thrown my paper into the dustbin and have no idea as to what it was about. At any rate, it was a huge success. I was immediately elected onto the committee for 1946. Then I was elected secretary for the five years 1950 to 1955.

This was really rather an important position. Indeed, most of my predecessors had become bishops. I had my hand on the pulse of all ecclesiastical intellectual activity in England and Wales. I got to know all the bishops, as some had a seminary in the diocese but others had a religious house of studies.

During those five years of 1950 to 1955, was there an organised "modernist" movement among the ecclesiastical intelligentsia? The answer is quite certainly no. Although a traditionalist myself, I am reasonably broad-minded. I should have allowed dissident papers to be read, since the conference could discuss "what it is not permitted to teach." Indeed, I invited a charming vernacular liturgist to have his say in 1951, but he was howled down. The ecumenists were more of a nuisance because Father Bevenot (an English Jesuit with a French name) was on the committee. He thought Anglicans so much nicer than Catholics. This may be so, but is quite beside the point. But I shall have to talk about ecumenicity later. There was a delightful Benedictine who refused to accept Pius XII's decree that the five ways prove the existence of

God. But he was a pure Wittgensteinian and influenced nobody but himself. I allowed a rather silly Dominican to talk heterodoxy, but he was immediately howled down by the Jesuits.

No, until Easter 1955, when I retired, the Catholic intelligentsia in England was not corrupt. The best proof of this is that in 1953 the Biblical Group of the Higher Studies Conference published a monumental Catholic Commentary on Holy Scripture. All its 1,300 pages are perfectly orthodox.

Being now in my eightieth year, names escape me. I forget the name of my successor in 1955. He was the professor of dogmatic theology at Wonersh. He resigned after only two years. He was a good and holy man. The reason he gave was that the job took too much time. Was this true, or was he running into difficulties in trying to contain the progressives?

While I was secretary I was very friendly with Canon Smith, the professor of theology at Ware. He was in fact German and his name was Schmidt. He read a perfectly orthodox paper for me at the Conference, but I had a certain reserve about him. His understudy was Charles Davies, of whom I was very fond. Now, it was I who proposed that Charles Davies be elected to the committee. In fact, I made his career. In succession to the Wonersh professor, Charles Davies was elected secretary to the Higher Studies Conference in 1958. It was then that it changed direction.

I forget the exact date: 1961? Father Clifford Howell S.J. had been asked to give a demonstration of the vernacular liturgy. The *pièce de résistance* was the tape-recording of a Mass in America with eight hundred people present. It seemed to me abysmal. When he had finished I got up and said: "Father Howell has completely changed the direction of the Catholic religion. The Mass, from being a divine activity, has become a human activity. From being theocentric, it has become anthropocentric." It must have been a divine inspiration. I am not clever enough to make that sort of remark out of the blue. It is true, and it remains the fundamental criticism of the new liturgies.

I was fond of Charles Davies as a man. At the Conference we were nearly always in the same clique after dinner. I realised that he was a bit progressive, but I had no idea how far it went.

He organised a meeting on ecumenicity. He could find crowds

of Anglicans and non-conformists but was hard put to finding a Jew and a Russian Orthodox. I suggested the famous Dominican and Jewish convert Jean de Menasce and an Orthodox bishop in London whom I knew.

Father de Menasce delivered perhaps the most brilliant lecture ever given at the Conference. It was dotting the i's and crossing the t's of his wonderful book *Quand Israël aime Dieu*. As for my Orthodox bishop, he probably repeated his Easter Sunday sermon! It was wonderfully orthodox and Charlie Davies was absolutely furious.

A curious event happened, I suppose in Easter 1964. There had been rather an amorphous paper on Teilhard de Chardin. Suddenly the secretary, Charlie, stood up and said: "I want to know if Father Houghton thinks that *The Phenomenon of Man* can be believed by a Catholic." I tried to ward off the question: "We already have one Apocalypse, which I find sufficiently difficult without having another." "That is not what I asked," said Charlie, and he repeated his question. "Very well, no. I think Teilhard de Chardin totally heterodox." As usual, he came over to my group after supper and drank my whisky. "Why were you so insistent about Teilhard this afternoon," I asked. He had probably had a few drinks already but he answered: "It's all the question of a mitre."

I never turned up to the Conference again. I believe it collapsed shortly afterwards, one of the earliest victims of the renewal.

Before I leave Slough, I have two curious events to record.

It was after the war, somewhere about 1951, because my Italian godchild Tono Mucchi was staying with me. At about two o'clock one morning a motorcyclist in the drive woke me up. He rang the bell. I answered him out of the window. "There is a lady who is dying at 239 Cedar Court," he said. "Could you come round immediately? I can take you on my bike."

"No, no; Cedar Court is next door and I can come on foot. But is the lady conscious? Should I bring her Holy Communion?"

"Yes, she's perfectly conscious alright."

I went down to the chapel, got the holy oils and Blessed Sacrament, and went over the road to 239 Cedar Court.

There was indeed a light burning in the front downstairs room of the house. I rang, and a woman answered the front door. I said I was the priest. She tried to stop me, but when carrying the Blessed Sacrament I talk to nobody. I pushed past her into the room where the light was burning. A woman was lying in bed, obviously a Catholic since she was saying the Rosary. She seemed a bit surprised and was not very cooperative. I ascribed that to the drugs she was taking. Anyway, I heard her confession, administered Extreme Unction and gave her Viaticum.

At about 7.00 a.m. the following morning the motorcyclist turned up again.

"Why didn't you come round last night? Anyway, you need not turn up as the old lady is alright."

"But I did go last night to 239 Cedar Court as you asked me to."

"No, I said 12 York Crescent."

Later in the course of the morning I passed in front of 239 Cedar Court. The undertakers were already there. It transpired that the woman whom I had anointed was a prostitute at a well-known house at Maidenhead. She was not very regular at Mass, but, as I had witnessed, she always said her Rosary.

Here is the second curious story.

The local secretary of the Communist Party was a Mr. T—call him Thomas, an English name. He asked to have his children admitted to my Catholic school—presumably because it was near where he lived. I refused. But he produced the baptismal certificate of his eldest boy in the name of Reardon—an Irish name. I made inquiries. Yes, Mr Thomas was really Mr Reardon, a baptised Irish Catholic. Well, I thought, I should get this matter straight. I turned up at lunchtime at Mr Thomas's home. I had prepared my speech: "Mr Thomas, I believe that you are really Mr Reardon and a baptised Catholic, validly married to a non-Catholic in a Catholic church, and that your eldest son is even a baptized Catholic. As your legitimate pastor, I ask you which identity you wish to assume. If you are Mr Reardon, your younger children will have to be baptized and you will have to renounce the Communist Party. If you are Mr Thomas, then you remain a communist. And I, as the legitimate representative of Holy Church, formally excommunicate you."

He lived in a council house. The dining room was not very large and he had little space in which to collect his thoughts. He was perfectly polite and understood the situation perfectly. Finally he said: "I am Mr Thomas. I remain secretary of the Communist Party. It is nearly two o'clock; I shall have to get back to work. Excuse me Father."

I watched him through the window get on his bike. His factory was not ten minutes from his home. But he never arrived there. He fell dead as he put his bicycle up in the rack. Heaven alone knows what had gone through his mind in the ten minutes between his home and the factory.

Mrs Thomas, a simple but good woman, came round to Wyvis Lodge to ask me to bury her husband. "Of course I'll bury him," say I.

It was in the cemetery of the Anglican church at Farnham Royal. I had prepared the service with some care, as it was the only chance I should ever have of addressing the Slough Communist Party. I turned up in a black cassock without surplice or stole. Unfortunately I have destroyed the text of the splendid service. It ran something like this—but lasted for a good twenty minutes:

"We are here to commemorate the death of George Thomas. He was baptized a Catholic and was brought up to worship his Creator and Redeemer. He denied them both. He thought he was created by evolution and redeemed by communism. So let it be! But listen to the sound of the leaves in the trees! It is not the rustle of leaves you hear, it is the sound of his soul sizzling in Hell. Yes, like you, he denied his Creator and Redeemer, and you can expect the same treatment as he, etc."

Instead of sprinkling holy water, I had collected a mass of stones which I had put in a basin on a stool. I proceeded to throw a stone at the head, feet and sides of the coffin. They landed with a great thump. I invited the congregation to do likewise, while I vanished to sign the registers. They were still throwing stones at the coffin when I left.

I thought I had been a bit hard on poor Mrs Thomas. After all, she was a perfectly decent woman. But I was much consoled by meeting her shortly afterwards in Slough High Street. "Oh Father!" she said, "thank you so much for that lovely ceremony!" In spite of the lovely ceremony I never managed to convert her, but she had the children baptised and I admitted them to the school.

I am up into the 1960s with the Higher Studies Conference, but I am still at Slough during the war.

The war duly ended in 1945, but the population in the North and South Farnham Wards scarcely diminished. This the government thought an excellent thing. The Battle for Britain proved that London was far too vulnerable: it needed to be dispersed. Slough would be a first dispersal area. This meant the compulsory purchase of Wyvis Lodge—heaven alone knows why.

It may be remembered that I bought Wyvis Lodge so as to be independent from the bishop. But in 1954 it became the property of London County Council. London offered me a five-year lease but I asked them to transfer the lease to the diocese so that the parish could continue. However, I did not relish the prospect of being a tenant at will of the bishop in my own house. I consequently paid rent, rates and taxes for five years in advance on Wyvis Lodge, but asked the bishop to move me elsewhere. He offered me Bury St Edmonds in Suffolk where the parish priest was dying. Indeed, I had to drive from Slough to bury him.

61

5

Bury St Edmunds

Bury St Edmunds was the exact opposite to Slough. It was an historic city with the ruins of a vast abbey where Magna Carta had been signed. My parish of Saint Anthony's, Slough, had been a couple of industrial wards of a mushroom town. Slough contained a few dormitory villages, whereas Bury, with a surface of nearly two hundred square miles, contained a quantity of real agricultural villages. There were practically no educated parishioners in Slough, whereas Bury was full of gentry, doctors, lawyers, civil servants, surveyors, accountants and what you will. However, the percentage of Catholics at Bury was low. Slough showed twelve and a half percent, while Bury St Edmunds showed only two percent in the villages and eight percent in the town.

The parish was in a good state spiritually thanks to two excellent curates, but was in a bad state physically. The parish priest whom I had buried had been a very good man, but he had already retired before the war. With the call-up of military chaplains he was asked to come back and take charge of the parish, but he was far too old to make decisions and look after property.

Among my parishioners was an ex-mayor of the city, who was still chairman of the water board. He assured me that Bury was sitting on enough water for sixty thousand inhabitants. But he was all in favour of keeping it a traditional market town of under twenty thousand. "My dear George," I said to him, "you haven't a chance. It is far cheaper to move people to the water than to move water to the people. Bury will inevitably become a town of sixty thousand. You must remember, besides, that water is going to become as precious as was petrol a few years back." Since I foresaw the growth of Bury, the schools became my primary pre-occupation, as they had been in Slough.

There was an all-age school. My predecessor had agreed to decapitate it, making it a primary school only. This agreement must obviously be quashed.

Clearly every Catholic child must attend a Catholic school. I consequently bought a bus and drove around myself to pick up the children from some of the more important villages. In this I was helped by my admirable curate Father Cureton who had driven buses during the war. Finally I hired buses to cover the whole area. Thanks to the loyalty of Catholic parents, we managed to swamp the school. Far from the all-age school being decapitated, two junior schools, one middle school and one senior school had to be built. It all represented a little heroism on the part of Catholic parents, of my curate—and of myself!

I shall never forget the journey to Honington one evening. It was a Friday, so we had to get rid of the children for the weekend. Snow had been falling since 3.00 p.m. By 4.00 p.m. some of the roads might be blocked. I rang up the police. Yes, the normal road to Honington via Ixworth was totally blocked, but I might get through on the road towards Thetford, as that was still open to traffic. I rang up Mr Grosz, a Catholic prisoner of war who had married an English girl: an admirable man. I knew that his working hours were from 4.00 a.m. to noon. "Will you help me try to get the school children back to Honington?," I asked. "I shall be with you within ten minutes."

We set off. The Thetford road out of Bury was alright. Lots of traffic had gone over it. But we came to the turning to Honington. The road was totally covered in snow. Mr Grosz said: "I'll get out and run in front of you. You try to run me down." He had a red beret, so he was easy to see. He must have run two miles through snow. We arrived at Honington. Cheers rose from some two hundred throats at the bus stop. Ours was the only bus which had got through from Bury. We delivered the odd thirty children to the delight of their parents.

But then, whom were we going to take back to Bury? Remember, it was Friday. Some two hundred men had weekend leave, but could not get away. I said that not more than forty-five were to be allowed to board, otherwise it would be too dangerous—and one man had to volunteer to run for two miles in front of the bus until we reached the Thetford road. Moreover, it was getting dark, and I had to have my forty-five within ten minutes. Luckily, there was some officer present who did not come himself but put forty-five men aboard. We delivered them at Bury station. How grateful I was to Mr Grosz!

Bury St Edmunds must be one of the very few towns in East Anglia to have had a Catholic priest resident from pre-Reformation times. When Thomas Garnet S.J. arrived as chaplain to the Rookewoods at Coldham Hall in about 1570 he found a Marian priest still alive at Bury. From Garnet's time onwards Bury became a Jesuit centre. There was even a Catholic school there during the Cromwellian period.

The very fine presbytery was built around 1765 by Father Gage S.J., the brother of the baronet of Hengrave and Coldham Halls. It had a fine chapel with a pretty frieze in Moorish Gothic which became my study. The splendid church was built by the Jesuits in neoclassical style immediately after Catholic emancipation in 1829.

Obviously, I restored the church and installed heating. It had been neglected since before the war. Also I had it consecrated. Although built in 1830/32 it had not been consecrated because it did not have a proper high altar. It merely had a temporary wooden frame on which was placed an altar stone.

Now it so happened that my friend George, the ex-mayor and chairman of the water board, owned some old houses in Bury. The tenancy of one became vacant and he decided to sell it. He first went over the house. There he found a splendid bath, cut out of one piece of Carrara marble in about 1830. It weighed five tons. He sold the house but kept the bath. He put it in his garden and planted some dwarf trees in it.

I saw it. "George," I said, "that is the ideal altar for the church. The original altars were sarcophagi of martyrs; a bath is also something into which you put a body. Moreover, it is of exactly the same date as the church." He let me have it. So I had a proper marble high altar and the church was duly consecrated.

I left Bury on November 29th, 1969. I write this page in April

1990. Obviously, few of my alterations remain—except the altar. Mind you, it is covered up so that it cannot be seen, but it is still there. The reason for this is quite simple. The church is built over a crypt with ordinary floorboards; it is not vaulted in stone or brick. Any attempt to move a monolith of five tons over the floorboards and out of the front door is far too great a risk. How, then, did I get it in? That was a little miracle—and I shall not tell you how I worked it.

As I have already mentioned, the real trouble with Bury parish was the odd twenty villages which surrounded it. Each one contained two or three Catholic families. Obviously, their children tended to get married in the Anglican churches—and their children could not be baptised Catholics because the Catholic parent had been excommunicated for attempting a sacramental marriage outside the Church. My general policy was quite clear. First, I should put the marriage right. Then I should baptise the children. Finally, I should bring the children into the Catholic schools at Bury and arrange a bus for Sunday Mass for the family. Incidentally, I left the care of the town to my curates and dealt with the villages myself. What staggered me in the villages was the loyalty of Catholics to the unique Church of Christ. Families where it was known that one deceased grandparent had been Catholic still wanted their children to be brought up in the religion. Anyway, the basis of my pastoral policy was to put the marriages right.

Well, it must have been in 1963 that I received a printed form from the bishop of Clifton. It required me to inscribe in my marriage register the marriage of a Catholic man from Clifton with an Anglican girl, which took place in the Anglican cathedral of Bury St Edmunds, without my even being informed. The celebrant was the bride's father, Canon X. of Bury cathedral. There were no promises in the file concerning the Catholic education of the children. All there was was a dispensation from Rome.

Needless to say, this event, much publicised in the local press, completely undermined my pastoral policy. However, by divine Providence, it came too late: the marriages in the villages had all been cleared up. But it warned me of the way things were evolving.

6

The Impact of the Council

The Council opened on October 11th, 1962. Up till then the Church seemed reasonably authoritative and exclusive. But from that moment onwards anything could be questioned. I forget the dates, but certainly vernacular liturgies were said in my deanery long before official permission was given in 1964. I managed to stop it for parochial Masses but not for private Masses. Experiment was in the air.

It was reported to me that one priest was saying Mass on weekdays in the presbytery dining-room, during breakfast, with consecrated toast. I immediately drove over to see him. I told him what had been reported to me.

"What's wrong with that?," he asked; "I am just trying to put a bit of reality and vitality into the Mass."

"Everything is wrong with it. Will you kindly say Mass with proper hosts and recognised wine according to the rubrics of 1962, just published, and on an altar in your church."

"Of course I shall, if you insist."

"I do insist."

"It's alright by me," he said, "and of course I would not offend you for worlds. You're a good guy; but you're barking up the wrong tree."

Mind you, I liked the priest in question. Unfortunately he landed up in a lunatic asylum after attempting to murder a very progressive bishop. He is a dear, good man—but a bit off balance.

Then, also in the early '60s, in a large house in the parish, there was a concelebrated Mass with a well-known Catholic priest, two Anglicans and two non-conformists. Everything had been perfectly arranged except that they had forgotten the hosts, so they had to send an employee into Bury to get them. That is how I heard about it.

Then there was Cardinal Bea's voyage to England to get the feel of the reaction of English Catholics towards ecumenicity. He was to meet two representatives of every diocese of England and Wales. I immediately wrote to the bishop proposing myself as a suitable delegate, since I was a convert from Anglicanism and ex-secretary of the Higher Studies Conference. He wrote back very apologetically, saying that Cardinal Bea's reception committee had decreed that he was not to meet a single convert during his stay in England, since they would all be prejudiced against their former confession! Is not that wonderful? That the totally ignorant are the only people who are totally unbiased!

Anyway, after permission for the vernacular liturgy in 1964, life became fairly intolerable. All the priests of my deanery, including my curate, turned to the vernacular. I remained alone. Out of 270 priests in the diocese, only four of us continued to say the old Mass. We canvassed the priests of the diocese to sign a petition that the bishop permit the old Mass. It is true that ninety priests signed it, but upon the bishop turning it down not one of them had the courage to say it.

The result in the parish was deplorable: the P. P. and curate said different Masses. I thought of retiring then and there. But I decided against [it]: the 1964 Mass had not touched the Canon— which in theory remained silent and in Latin. It was still possible to say the 1964 Mass with a certain amount of devotion. However, I wrote to the bishop handing in my resignation the day on which the Canon of the Mass was touched. He wrote back a charming letter in which he says: "Nobody intends to reform the Canon," and that "the bishops are there precisely to preserve it." Poor, dear Bishop! Little did he know what was going to happen. But I knew. Not only had I my friends of the Higher Studies Conference, but I picked up some interesting gossip at the Missions de France at Moissac. Also, I had reason to visit the Canisianum at Innsbruck where I had an informal chat with Karl Rahner and Jungmann. Both were most enlightening.

But there was a problem to which I found an answer difficult. All priests had said the old Mass daily and with due decorum and

even with apparent devotion. How came it that ninety-eight percent were perfectly willing to change it—and this not at the
behest of the Council or of the Pope? A pure permission was
given, and they all jumped to it like the Gadarene swine. Besides,
I had been dean for a number of years and knew the priests of my
deanery very well. Only two of them were sufficiently stupid to
think themselves brilliant—and consequently welcomed the
opportunity to express their personality. The rest, in private, were
against the changes. However, only one, a Dominican, stuck to
the old Mass. What made the others change? Obedience, apathy,
fear of reprisals, anything for a quiet life—all those sorts of
motives undoubtedly played their part, but the fact remains that
they cannot have *loved* the old Mass. It was just a ritual which
could be changed like a pair of pants. But if they did not love the
Mass it must be that they were incapable of adoration. They must
consider Mass as something they do, not as something God does.

"Lex credendi, lex orandi"—faith rules prayer and prayer faith.
I had no doubt about the faith of my fellow priests—except one,
perhaps—so the trouble must lie with prayer. Here, indeed, I
found us priests singularly lacking. We were much too busy saying Mass, saying our breviary or doing something, to spend a
moment in prayer in front of the Blessed Sacrament. We encouraged the laity to do so, but rarely did it ourselves. Now I come to
think of it, during my seminary course at the Beda I received
plenty of instruction on ascetics, on how to perfect myself; but
none on prayer, how to adore God. What little I know about the
adoration of God I had picked up by reading the mystics—such
as Gertrude of Helfta and Teresa of Avila—or spiritual writers
such as Augustine Baker, Surin and Grou.

Now, it is clear that ascetics, directed as it is towards self-perfection, requires intelligent human acts, aided by God's "actual
grace." On the other hand, prayer, which is the pure adoration of
God, is the fruit of habitual or sanctifying grace; it is the return of
the love of the Holy Ghost to the Father through the medium of
a human being. Humanly speaking, it is an act of the will bent on
self-emptying, recollection, adherence, in order to adore God.

I think that once one has got the distinction between ascetics
and prayer clearly in mind, the revolution in the Church becomes

comprehensible. Priests—and above all really successful priests, i.e., bishops—became fed up with a liturgy in which they had nothing to do. They wanted an ascetical instead of an adorational Mass—activity instead of contemplation. This is exactly what they have got.

I wrote a paper on this subject called "Prayer, Grace and the Liturgy," which I first read before Christmas in 1965 at Nottingham University. Since then it has been the rounds. It has been published in the U.S.A. and in Italy, but not in England or France.

Here it is. I think it a bit boring and pedantic, but I publish it because I think it has a certain importance. Firstly, because it happens to be true. Secondly, after twenty-five years, nobody has taken it up. Thirdly, we still suffer from an active instead of a contemplative Mass.

7

Prayer, Grace & the Liturgy

It is now nearly three years since the vernacular was introduced into the Mass. Its introduction, if not its consequences, is a matter of history which can be viewed with a certain amount of detachment. That it was an event of the utmost importance none can deny: *lex orandi, lex credendi*. Faith rules prayer and prayer faith. Besides, strangely superficial would he be who maintained that several million people could be made to change overnight the millennial atmosphere of their spiritual lives without its being in any way significant. Never, perhaps, has there been so drastic a change in the form of worship of a religion which claimed to be the same after as before.

Neither has the change been restricted to language. The position of the altar, of the tabernacle, of the priest; the gestures of the celebrant, the movements of the congregation—all have changed. Illuminating as it would be to analyse these in detail, it would lengthen inordinately the present paper. Besides, in some measure, they all seem subordinate to the same proposition: that no symbol is significant other than the intelligible spoken word. The problem of the vernacular liturgy can therefore be said to include them.

To the historian, the right or wrong of the change is immaterial. The problem is, why it should occur when it did instead of in a different context at a different time. What is there peculiar to Advent 1964 which was absent in Advent 964? Then, how comes it that the same bishop should proscribe one day what he prescribes the next? The same applies to a priest, ordained in and for the Latin Mass, who has celebrated it every day for years, explained it and defended it whenever he instructed a convert, preached it from his pulpit: how comes it that he can jettison it without a thought, or even inveigh against it without a blush? A few bishops or priests here and there, under particular circumstances and in particular places, would present no problem. But it is the hierarchy everywhere, and so large a majority of priests, that any protest is inaudible. Neither can it be maintained that the clergy were forced into it by overwhelming popular demand. It is a matter of historical fact that the diverse national vernacular societies of pre-conciliar days were not only clearly clergy-sponsored but almost entirely clerical in membership, and they tended, moreover, to exclude the Mass from their programmes. On the other hand, the Latin Mass Society is perhaps the only spontaneous, entirely lay organization of Catholic action in the Church.

Since it would be absurd to maintain that all bishops and the majority of priests are knaves or fools, a sufficient cause must be sought to explain a change at once so abrupt and so universally acclaimed. Somehow, somewhere, there must have been building up, quite unconsciously, an attitude of mind inimical to the Latin Mass. Its vast monolithic structure appeared intact, but it can only have been standing by sheer force of habit. It must have been undermined. At the press of a button it collapsed. Yes, but who pressed the button, and who had bored the galleries, and when?

These are problems for the historian to probe, if not to answer. They are outside the purview of the liturgician or theologian, who provide the matter for the history.

In viewing these momentous changes, it must be remembered that the avowed reasons are not necessarily the real ones, partly because the problem may not be what people think so much as why they should think it, partly because the reasons given are likely to be *post hoc* rationalisations of deeper, perhaps inexplicable, feelings. If this is true of the Protestant Reformation or of the French Revolution, it may be equally so of the reform of the liturgy. Nevertheless, the avowed reasons deserve consideration.

First for the Latinist.[1] What reasons does he advance for the

---

1 That is, a proponent of the Latin Mass.

retention of a largely inaudible and usually incomprehensible liturgy? He complains of the irreparable loss of a symbol of unity in time and place. He points out the absurdity of an Englishman in Rome hunting out his tribal church; the inevitable conflicts arising from the vernacular in multi-linguistic societies; the positive danger to the Church of colonial languages in emancipated countries. Not only are the translations unsatisfactory, but it is childish to imagine that a vernacularised liturgy has been created by merely translating Latin, since each language has its proper genius, and the English equivalent of a Latin epigram would be a purple passage from Macauley. Anyway, not only is silence highly significant, but alone it is common to all languages. Then, there is the insoluble problem of music, etc.

Reasons such as these are objectively true, valid and weighty, but it may reasonably be doubted whether they are the real ones why the Latinist hates the vernacular. They are too accidental. Supposing English were declared the universal language of the Church, and the Mass, not translated but rewritten in impeccable and harmonious English, were celebrated by the least inadequate of priests, would the Latinist accept it? Of course he wouldn't! It would still grate on his innermost soul. Still he would suffer agony.

If hard pressed, however, the Latinist usually advances a quite different sort of reason. It is rather variously and often inadequately expressed—a hopeful sign, because abstract arguments are always clear, whereas reality is never totally expressible. It runs something like this: "The Mass has lost its anonymity. In the old Mass the priest was insignificant; now his every word is intentionally significant. And, since he speaks my language, which I cannot help but understand, he impinges on me. To pray is impossible, because my native tongue does not merely cause me distractions, it is itself the distraction. Even worse, I too have lost my anonymity. In the old Mass, I did not count; now I must express myself, and do it in community. I used to be recollected; now I must be active: these cannot be reconciled. In the old Mass heart spoke to heart, *cor ad cor loquitur*; now that the Mass is audible, it is the heart which is silent. There is no devotion left."

Such a view may appear rather subjective, but it has the enormous advantage of ringing true. It is likely to be a genuine pointer to the real reasons underlying the Latinist's attitude. Incidentally, it would go a long way to explain the undeniable phenomenon that the people who know Latin least are usually those who most lament its departure. To them the hieratic tongue was a positive help towards anonymity; to a professor well acquainted with the language, Latin was directly significant and might as well be English.

What then of the vernacularist's avowed reasons? There is one which can be dismissed straightaway as inadequate: that the Mass provides the natural opportunity for the Church to fulfil her teaching mission. Has nobody ever thought of preaching a sermon during Mass? What precisely does it teach a person to mumble, year in, year out, "Lord, have mercy," rather than to listen to *Kyrie, eleison*? Besides, is it even true that "the Lord be with you" means the same as *Dominus vobiscum*? Does it in fact produce the same mental images and carry the same associations? Anyway, apart from the theory, in practice would the fact that his congregation was composed exclusively of *periti* who had nothing to learn prevent the vernacularist from saying his vernacular Mass? Of course it would not; on the contrary.

A far more interesting line of thought, although equally unlikely to be the sufficient cause for such momentous changes, is the vernacularist's revivalism, the "back to the primitives" common to all revolutions. The fact is that from time to time societies seem to reach such a state of perfection that people grow heartily sick of them. The techniques appear too slick and the content too slim. The reaction is not to increase the content but to break the container: "back to the primitives!" In 1520, what could medieval Germany produce after the Hallenkirche? What was one to carve after Riemenschneider? "Back to the Bible," before churches were built or images carved. In the France of the Ancient Regime, what could one do other than break it up? "Back to the virtue of Republican Rome!" It is perhaps not unfair to say that in this storm-tossed age the Barque of Peter seemed a little too secure. If the waves could not rock it, then the sailors could. It rode the sea with a triumphalism which exasperated: "our Faith, that is the triumphant principle which triumphs over the world!" (1 John 5:4).

Well, it mustn't; the Barque should be made to ship a bit of water. And the crew was governed by the imperturbable rule of Canon Law; a little caprice, a touch of anarchy must immediately be introduced. "Back to the primitive Church!"

Of course, it is not the first revival to which the Church has been subjected. Indeed, the Gothic revival has scarcely ended, so that the same priest who maintained a few years since that the conversion of England was a matter of rood screens, riddle curtains, apparelled amices, plainchant and scholasticism is now as convinced that a facing altar, the simplest stole, much Bible-reading, a community Mass and existentialism will convert the world. What is curious about the present case is the period which it has chosen to revive.

The extraordinary resemblance between the declines of the West and of Imperial Rome, between our own age and that of Saint Augustine, has long since been recognised. It comes therefore as rather a shock that anybody should revive deliberately the Christianity of the fourth to sixth centuries. Yet that is precisely the period chosen. Like all revivals, it is, of course, highly selective. Just as one caught the Flying Scotsman from a Gothic station or ate with Victorian silver from a Gothic refectory table, so is it the religious socialism of its public worship which alone is revived from the age of Saint Augustine. Not for imitation are the far more significant religious phenomena of the identical period, provided by the Stylites and the monks of the new Thebaid, by those, in fact, whom the religious socialism of their age drove into the desert or, quite literally, up the wall. But, if these extreme forms of religious individualism have not been selected for imitation, it does not follow that they will not emerge. A distinguished author has written in a private letter concerning the changes: "I have to remind myself that the Church's affair is to carry the deposit of faith through the ages, and that her witness in temples is only a part—from henceforward perhaps a diminishing part— in her destiny... The one good effect is that more of us will be driven into Saint Teresa's Interior Castle, where God can talk in his own language of silence." He is ripe for the desert.

But, no matter how fascinating a revival may be, how illustrative of a movement, it can never be its cause.

No, the basic justification for the vernacular Mass is, as the vernacularists themselves proclaim, participation. The trouble with it is that the word is very ambiguous. Sharing what, how, and with whom? To have shares in a limited liability company, to take part in a conversation, to take part in a play, imply rather different meanings in the word participation itself.

Then there are two quite distinct levels at which a person might be thought to participate: the ecclesial (as a member of the Church) and the personal. It may be as well to point out straight away that an intelligible liturgy does not affect the former. The baby who understands nothing and screams its own variety of vernacular throughout the Mass participates on the ecclesial level just as effectively as the celebrant, since it is a member of the Church, and the Church is equally present under any one of its members, just as Jesus Christ is equally present under any one Host. It is on the personal level that the baby is as good as, or worse than, absent. It follows that the participation which an intelligible liturgy has in view must take place on the personal level. Yes, but with whom? Who is the other "party" to the participation?

It can scarcely be maintained that the other party is God. Although the remark may appear a little facetious, it nonetheless remains true that the one Person who obstinately refuses to participate in an audible, vernacular Mass is God; on His side, He continues to utter no more than the Word made flesh. Anyway, if participation with God is in any sense contingent on an audible, vernacular liturgy, then everywhere and for over a thousand years the Church has encouraged and taught an inadequate system of attendance at the Sacred Mysteries. If that is so, in what can the Church be trusted, since she cannot be in what is her primary concern: religion itself, the participation of man with God?

If it cannot be God, then is the other party to the participation the priest and one's fellow worshippers? At first sight it looks as though it is. Canon J.B. O'Connell in the Redemptorist Pamphlets writes: "It is almost incredible to think that for a thousand years the vital link between the worshipping people in the benches and the ministers at the altar had been cut." It is here implied audible vernacular activity constitutes the vital link between worshippers and ministers, not the recollected attention of the congregation which may always have been there. But is it quite as simple as that? If it cannot be doubted but that some people derive a psychological benefit from community prayer, neither can it be but that many do not. Far from introducing a rich sense of belonging, of corporateness, in a congregation, it has brought about a cleavage inconceivable before its introduction. Besides, such a view of participation is inadequate to explain all the facts. Why, for instance, should convents of women be specifically singled out for the vernacular Mass? The spiritual state of most nuns is at least the prayer of simple regard; the vernacular Mass is more likely to cause them exquisite agony than to increase their community spirit. They probably have already rather too many community prayers; to add the Mass to the list seems a bit churlish. Or again, on weekdays in small churches, the mere fact that none of the devout souls present attempt to join in, and all are known to be confirmed Latinists, will not prevent a priest so minded from saying a vernacular Mass. He is not of necessity a sadist, but the reason for his saying it must of necessity be other than to restore the "vital link between the worshipping people in the benches and the ministers at the altar."

If participation as a sufficient cause for vernacular liturgy cannot mean sharing with God, and does not quite mean taking part with priest and neighbour, then it may mean "taking a part": enacting, in fact, rather than sharing. This seems to be so. No matter how well a person may know Latin, he does not normally think in it; he does not express himself in it, above all to himself; it remains artificial. He may know the meaning of *Agnus Dei*, but there is no personal involvement—it is as though another were speaking; whereas "Lamb of God" has a real meaning to him, implies a personal commitment. Even if the congregation simply won't answer up, the priest, with heroic determination, will still say the vernacular Mass, still commit himself in the language which is meaningful to him. If the congregation does answer up, then it is from the sum of these personal commitments that springs the exhilaration of participation with one's neighbour, Canon O'Connell's "vital link." The dialogued Latin Mass was absolutely inadequate for this purpose. It merely multiplied the servers from two to two hundred, perhaps; but mere servers they remained, uninvolved, uncommitted, impersonal, anonymous, by the mere force of the hieratic tongue. In their own tongue, however, they speak meaningfully. No longer are they servers but persons, not slaves but free men, the People of God.

If this brief analysis of the avowed reasons of Latinist and vernacularist for holding their positions bears any resemblance to the truth, then the point at issue has been fairly precisely defined. The Latinist looks for self-effacement, anonymity, in the Mass; the vernacularist for self-commitment, inanonymity. They are irreconcilable.

But, if the point at issue has been clearly defined, the problem remains how a head-on collision has occurred in a religion so dogmatic and so unified as the true Church. Before examining the possibilities, one simple explanation must be excluded: that it is a matter of temperament—the Latinists are introverts, seeking to lose themselves even in public worship; the vernacularists are extroverts, wishing to impress their personality even on the Mass. Would that it were so, but it does not fit the facts! Who does not know an introvert vernacularist or extrovert Latinist? It is really very funny to think of some of the Renaissance popes as desperate introverts. And what made everybody become introverted in the mid-twentieth century? Such an explanation will not work. What is true, of course, is that, irrespective of his temperament, for a man to pray he must be capable of a modicum of introversion. The still, small voice is not suitable for the microphone. But that is rather a different matter.

Lex orandi, lex credendi. There are only two reasons why liturgies should change: because beliefs have changed—the *lex credendi*—or because the attitude to prayer has changed—the *lex orandi*. It was consequently perfectly right that at the time of the Reformation the Protestants should have changed the liturgy. Had they not done so, they would have been hypocrites. Has there been a change of belief in the Catholic Church such as would affect the liturgy of the Mass?

This is not a matter on which an historian can as yet give a valid opinion. The intellectual brew is still in the process of fermentation and cannot yet be bottled, labelled and presented to the historian. One must proceed with caution. It has been stated, for instance, that sixty percent of the theological students at a major Austrian seminary do not believe in the Real Presence in any recognisable form. But is it true? Perhaps sixty percent of the mind of the interviewer could not recognise the form in which the theological students believed in the Real Presence. It is at least possible.

Undeniably, however, there have been certain changes in emphasis, and it has not been sufficiently borne in mind that in words of more than one syllable such as "refuse" or "desert" the meaning depends entirely on which is emphasised. Two of these changes seem worth mentioning, one negative, one positive. Negatively, "transubstantiation" has become almost as dirty a word as "triumphalism" or "canon law." The reason is philosophical and may have little or nothing to do with theology. But the result is that the pastoral clergy, whose belief in the Real Presence is a sound as a bell, have nonetheless lost a term which was perfectly meaningful to them and which has not been replaced. They consequently find themselves speechless on the central mystery of the Christian faith.

More important is the positive change. A number of scholars with a considerable following among the clergy would not deny the Real Presence, but believe it to be an abuse of that Presence to use it apart from the communal event of the People of God actively participating (enacting) in the Lord's Supper—the Mass. As with their dislike of the term "transubstantiation," the basis for this view is an existential instead of an ontological philosophy.

Few, however, would carry this existential view to its extreme, although logical, conclusion: that outside the event of the Mass the Real Presence has no meaning and therefore no existence.

Such an attitude explains a great deal that has happened, is happening and will probably come to be in Catholic churches. The Blessed Sacrament has been removed from the high altar by the simple expedient of turning the altar round. It is still reserved, but as discreetly as possible, to avoid the abuse of private devotion. It would be preferable not to reserve at all but to deposit unconsumed Hosts in the sacrarium, especially as Viaticum is clearly undesirable since it militates against the proper use of the sacrament of Anointing. It is not difficult to find churches which are locked outside of the times of services, although there is nothing in them to steal or to desecrate. A surprising number of the clergy are already hesitant about saying private Masses, especially during the holidays, and such Masses are unlikely to survive for long. The current attack against Mass stipends may be seen as a means to wean the clergy from their vested interest in preserving such Masses. Indeed, concelebration was not very popular until all co-celebrants could take a stipend. In practice, Benediction has been abolished by the introduction of the evening Mass, coupled with the recent decree forbidding its celebration before or after Mass. Corpus Christi processions are grinding to a halt, and the Forty Hours will be quietly dropped. Apart, perhaps, from some form of "study group services," the Mass alone will remain, but the Real Presence, instead of being the centre of all Christian devotion, must become a meaningful "event." This last idea is excellently expressed in a recent pastoral of one of our English bishops: "Up to now most of us have spent the quiet time between the Sanctus and the Our Father waiting for the coming of our Lord... so that we might adore him truly present in the Blessed Sacrament... The church is taking away from us this quiet . . . not because she does not think the kind of prayer valuable and necessary, but because she thinks that the time of the Canon is not the best time for it"—that is, for the adoration of our Lord in the Blessed Sacrament. Inevitably, since the bishop concerned is honourable and devout, he continues by recommending the desert: "Our Blessed Lord Himself gives us both teaching and example about this. He said: But when you pray go to your private room..." Yes, precisely, you cannot, nay must not, pray in church. It need come as no surprise if the churches tend to be empty.

That this change of emphasis in the *lex credendi* has provided the driving force for the introduction of vernacular liturgies seems undeniable. Nevertheless, it does not explain all the facts. An existentialist, activist view of the Blessed Sacrament is consciously held by a small minority of the pastoral clergy, although it may be more common among intellectual regulars. The overwhelming majority hold a very traditional view of the Mass and of the Real Presence. If, then, they have welcomed the vernacular, it is certainly not because they subscribe to any change of emphasis in belief. They would probably be deeply shocked if they thought there was any connection between the two. Since this is so, then the real reason for the momentous changes which we have all witnessed is to be sought elsewhere. This does not mean that the *Zeitgeist*, so admirably illustrated in the change of emphases in the *lex credendi*, is unimportant; but what it does mean is that it must have found the ground singularly well prepared for it to have been sown, to have grown, flowered and fructified, like some rare desert flower, almost overnight.

Has there been a change, then, in the *lex orandi*, in the theory and practice of prayer? Indeed there has, and a change so subtle, taking place over so many hundreds of years, that it has passed almost unperceived.

The traditional view, accepted universally up to the Reformation and in the Catholic Church up to today, is that Christian prayer is an act of habitual, sanctifying grace. That is to say, that the prayer of a Christian differs from the equivalent act in a Stoic or a Buddhist not merely in its content or object but in its essence. Whereas Stoic or Buddhist is performing a natural act, aided and abetted by actual grace, the Christian is aiding and abetting a supernatural act performed by the Holy Ghost. The two processes are clean contrary; the former is a human act sanctified, the latter a divine act humanised.

Since the Holy Ghost is the operator and the human being merely the co-operator in Christian prayer, it follows inexorably that it is the one act which can only be done in a state of grace. A man may receive Holy Communion sacrilegiously, but he cannot pray sacrilegiously. Therefore, either he must take some pains to be in a state of grace or if, after grievous sin, he is conscious of being in a state of prayer, then he must have made some act equivalent to perfect contrition, because to pray he must be in a state of grace. In practice, the traditional view prefers the former alternative: a little trouble should be taken to be in a state of grace. Hence the importance attached to what the ancients called "temperance," later writers "mortification" and the moderns "ascetics," that is the practice of the virtues and of pious meditation. But the practice of ascetics is not of itself formally prayer. What it does is to provide the circumstance in which prayer is normally possible. It is true that a meditation may be a prayer, but it will be so not by the thing thought out by the intention, because human cooperation with the Holy Ghost is not an act of the intelligence but an act of the will.

Thus, the thoughts which a priest expresses in a sermon or a professor of theology in his lecture are not prayers. They remain exactly what they pretend to be: true, beautiful and pious thoughts. A preacher may indeed move himself to prayer by his own sermon, but as soon as he does so he will have to stop preaching, unless, like the Curé d'Ars, he is in an habitual state of prayer. The activity of the human being in prayer is something quite different: it is the adherence to grace, and the less he impinges on the Holy Ghost the better. This he does not by pious thoughts and good resolutions, which would remain "his" thoughts and "his" resolutions—all forms of self-centeredness— but by here and now being self-effacing, abandoning all that is "his," to become as theocentric as grace permits. He should become recollected and empty himself so as to leave room for the divine operation of the Holy Ghost. Although petition, propitiation and thanksgiving have their place in prayer, its final note is adoration, the *amour pur* of the Fénélon-Bossuet controversy, the very thing which, according to the episcopal text already quoted, is now considered an improper activity during the Canon of the Mass.

In the traditional view it is hotly denied that its theocentricity is in any way antisocial. On the contrary. All one's pious self-exhortations and resolutions to love one's neighbour might help one to be reasonably polite to him and to exercise well-intentioned hypocrisy, but they could not make one love him because they remain mere human acts. But real prayer, in which the person forgets his neighbour as himself only to adhere to God, would so perfect him that, to his own surprise, he might suddenly distinguish in that neighbour something loveable and before unseen. This is the operation of grace.

Neither must it be imagined that such a view of prayer may be descriptive of high contemplatives in the unitive way but cannot be applied to the simple faithful. This is not true. All the forms of prayer peculiar to and encouraged by the Church imply and require a state of recollection and adherence, not of meaningful commitment and activity. The Rosary, the Litanies, the Stations, the Divine Praises, the indulgenced ejaculations, who has ever thought of the words spoken or even of the particular mystery? In what possible way are such repetitions meaningful? Their use is to reduce the activity of the human mind to a minimum in order to liberate the soul for adherence to God in prayer.

Granted such a philosophy of prayer, the position of the Latinist is seen to be perfectly rational. He will attend Mass with a Rosary, a *Garden of the Soul*, the *Imitation of Christ*, a missal or nothing at all—with whatever experience teaches him will keep him recollected in himself and attentive to the adorable Presence. This desire for anonymity, for recollection, in order to adore Jesus Christ truly present in the Blessed Sacrament is not personal preference born of habit, but is an integral part of his innermost belief. The vernacularist need not hold that from the Desert Fathers down to Dom John Chapman all Catholics everywhere were unaccountably obtuse. They may have held a wrong philosophy of prayer, but at any rate their liturgy exemplified it perfectly.

That the traditional philosophy of prayer was unacceptable to the Protestant Reformers—especially to Calvin—is obvious enough. It was not only the Mass which went, but the whole system of Catholic prayer, because the Reformers held a different system of grace. An analysis of the numerous Protestant liturgies would be deeply interesting but is outside the scope of the present paper. What is to the point is when and how the attitude altered among Catholics.

The late Henri Brémond ascribed the change to the *Exercises* of Saint Ignatius. Whatever the nature of Saint Ignatius' own prayer, the constant repetition of the *Exercises*, especially as propounded in Rodriguez's *Perfection*, could not fail to give the impression that prayer was essentially a human act, dependent like any other on actual grace, not a supernatural act, dependent on the Holy

Ghost through habitual sanctifying grace. To pray, one had to choose a subject for meditation, imagine compositions of time and place, draw conclusions, produce affections, make resolutions. Moreover, the object of the exercise was anthropocentric— one's own perfection—and not theocentric—the adoration of God. The result, to Brémond, was the exact opposite of prayer: instead of activity of the will bent on self-emptying, recollection and adherence, in order to adore God, there is the maximum intellectual and imaginative activity directed towards self-perfection. It is the substitution of ascetics for prayer, of the means for the end. A lyrical professor of theology would infallibly pray best, and it would remain a profound mystery how anybody as stupid as the Little Flower or Bernadette Soubirous ever prayed at all.

The unifying principle in Brémond's vast literary output is the illustration of this thesis. Among ten thousand others he produces one quotation so formidable that no one interested in this problem can afford to neglect it. In 1923 a certain Father Vincent published a work called *François de Sales directeur d'âmes et éducateur de la volonté* (Brémond's *Introduction à la philosophie de la prière*, Bloud & Gay, 1929). Here are some relevant passages: "If we see God as the Jews saw Him in His disturbing majesty, shall we not be inclined to prostrate ourselves before Him and consequently to subordinate all our religious duties to that of adoration and praise? If man conceives of God in the Jewish manner, he will tend to forget himself, lose sight of self, so as somehow to perceive nothing but the omnipotent Master. If, on the other hand, God is thought of as a father or an indulgent tutor, anxious to adorn our souls, infallibly we shall be led to centre our preoccupation on ourselves." Father Vincent then proceeds to show that if the adorational tradition lasted for some fifteen hundred years, this was due to the early Fathers being impregnated with Judaism and their attitude being perpetuated by the Benedictines. This last statement was true enough when Dom John Chapman was Abbot of Downside, but Bishop Butler might find it a bit hard on him. "Liturgical asceticism," Father Vincent continues, by which comic term he means the traditional view of prayer, "liturgical asceticism which, as has been seen, has its origin way beyond the Gospel, right back in the old Mosaic law, and which is based on a reverential awe of the divinity, remains the norm up to the sixteenth century." At last the Jesuits come with their "higher conception of religion." They understood that God "thirsts more for our spiritual progress than our praise." At last they "identified Christianity with moral progress." Their "invariable and primary preoccupation" was to honour God *première- ment par la culture de soi, secondement par la culture des autres*— "firstly by self-improvement and then by improving one's neighbours." The praise of God is doubtless excellent, "but only insofar as it contributes to our growth. Of itself it is nothing, unless we reduce it to its proper instrumental function, unless we make it a means of (self-) perfection and an instrument of love (towards our neighbour)."

Whether Father Vincent's historical appreciations concerning Jews and Jesuits are true or false is quite beside the point; anyway, they will be referred to later. What is undeniable is that his philosophy of prayer represents a total revolution, and completely justifies Brémond's diagnosis. It is equally undeniable that it is this philosophy of prayer which justifies the vernacular liturgy. If prayer can be equated with "moral progress," if it is a human act, dependent on actual grace like any other, and directed towards self-perfection, then of course there should be an intelligible, vernacular, didactic liturgy, which the worshipper can "enact," which he can understand, in which he can express himself, involve and commit himself. Perhaps the vernacularist holds a wrong philosophy of prayer, but at any rate his liturgy exemplifies it perfectly.

Beyond any reasonable doubt, this is the sufficient cause for the momentous changes we have witnessed in the liturgy. The change of emphasis in the *lex credendi* may have sparked off the explosion, but the vast monument of the Latin Mass had previously been undermined by a slow and silent change in the *lex orandi*, the doctrine of grace as it affects prayer.

It remains to be seen how this slow and silent change came about. Both Brémond and Vincent ascribed it to the Jesuits, the one to their damnation, the other to their glory. Plausible as it appears, it will not fit the facts.

Whatever the *Exercises* were taken to be at a later date, in the sixteenth and seventeenth centuries they were thought to be exercises, a form of spiritual drill, of high ascetics in fact. They were not thought of as a manual of prayer. How Saint Ignatius prayed can best be judged by the fact that he had to get a dispensation from Office "because the performance thereof took up almost the whole day, so abundant were the divine visitations in it towards him" (Augustine Baker, *Sancta Sophia* III, S. 1, chap. vii, par. 28). Under such circumstances he would be unlikely to get very far with the *Exercises* as a method of prayer. Then there is Saint Teresa's confessor, Father Balthazar Álvarez, who deliberately abandoned the *Exercises*. Of course busybodies reported him to the General, but the fact remained that he vindicated himself completely and was later entrusted with the highest offices the Society had to offer him. More curious is the case of Rodriguez's *Perfection*, as it illustrates the different spirit in which books get read at different times. To Brémond in the twentieth century it is the cause of all the trouble, yet it is precisely among the list of recommended books given by Dom Augustine Baker, that champion of traditional spirituality in the early seventeenth century. One could go on indefinitely. The fundamental attitude of the Society before its suppression in these matters can best be judged, however, by whose side it took when it came to the crunch in the Fénelon-Bossuet controversy: as is well known, Fénelon's defence was organised by Father Dez from the Gesù. No, the origin of the new spirituality must be sought elsewhere. The honour or infamy cannot lie with the Society.

On the face of it, a new philosophy of prayer is only likely to arise as a by-product of a new theory of grace. It is the Jansenists, not the Jesuits, who produced one. It is interesting to notice that they too were revivalists of the fourth to sixth centuries, but they went further than the moderns and even revived the Thebaid, a desert for intellectuals at Port Royal des Champs. But what is more to the point, their theory of "sufficient grace" cut right across the traditional view of prayer, because it denied the existence of sanctifying grace on which that view depends. "Sufficient grace" is always concerned with acts, whereas sanctifying grace is concerned with a state. In many respects the Jansenists were existentialists before their time. As a natural consequence of such a theory, if anyone ever "identified Christianity with moral progress" and prayer with "self-improvement," it was the Jansenists.

The new spirituality was injected into the Church by no less a person than the great Bossuet. Even though he may not have been a Jansenist himself, his theologian, Nicole, certainly was. Although he did not subscribe to the theory of sufficient grace, he must have felt a natural attraction to their attitude to prayer. Bossuet was precisely a lyrical theologian, one who probably lectured God on theology in his prayer, just as his theological writings are sublimated by a unique flow of lyricism. Whatever the true origins of the Quietest controversy, and they will probably forever be shrouded in darkness, there can be no doubt but that the Jansenists, via Nicole, used Bossuet to attack traditional spirituality by means of Madame Guyon. The target was not really that pious, intelligent lady who scribbled too much, but *amour pur*, disinterested love, pure adoration—precisely what is now declared unsuitable for the Canon of the Mass. Fénélon sprang to the defence of traditional spirituality. The outcome was the Articles of Issy, in which Bossuet capitulated all along the line. But the matter was not going to be allowed to rest there. Fénélon, quite understandably but perhaps unwisely, knocked off a perfectly anodyne but not very good little book to explain the Articles—the *Maximes des Saints*. Eagles have notoriously good sight, and the Eagle of Meaux managed to see in the work errors "to shake the very foundations of Christianity." The outcome is well known. After a Roman commission had sat for one hundred and thirty-two sessions over a period of two years, twenty-three quite secondary propositions were condemned by Innocent XII, but the general thesis of *amour pur* was not. In fact, as Cardinal [Louis-François] de Bausset has pointed out, Fénélon triumphed in his condemnation.

Yes, but neither the powers that be, nor Bossuet nor the Jansenists were going to let it appear so. Fénélon is condemned, so his whole system, the traditional spirituality which he upheld, must be wrong. The result was immediate. While the seventeenth century was probably the richest there has ever been in spiritual writers, the eighteenth is certainly the poorest. Nobody dared to pray, let alone write about it.

Fénélon was condemned on March 12th, 1699. Immediately the Age of Reason, of irreligion, sets in. In less than a hundred years there are bishops like Loménie de Brienne and Talleyrand, the Civil Constitution of the Clergy is proclaimed, clerical celibacy abolished and the vernacular Mass introduced in over eighty of the hundred and thirty-five French dioceses.

Honour must be given where it is due. In the religious collapse of the eighteenth century, one religious order held out conspicuously for traditional spirituality. It was not the Benedictines, *pace* Father Vincent, but the Jesuits. They went down with their colours flying. Caussade and Grou are not only the finest spiritual writers of the century, but the latter perhaps the finest the Society has ever produced.

The Society was suppressed in 1773. It was revived forty-one years later. It is a long time, more than a generation. Where Brémond and Vincent may be right is that the restored Society seems to have had a slightly different outlook on prayer to the old Society. It is, of course, very difficult to revive the spirit and easier to revive the letter—but it is "the spirit that quickeneth." Nobody denies there having been great spirituals in the Society over the past hundred and fifty years; we have all met some, in our own personal experience. But it is also difficult to deny two propositions: i. that many individual Jesuits today are to the forefront in introducing the precise form of spirituality which the old Society fought to the bitter end; ii. that the new spirituality has been propagated, partly by an improper use of the *Exercises*, in clergy retreats. This latter statement, if true, would go a long way to explain why the clergy, not the laity, are particularly prone to the new outlook.

The present paper will have fulfilled its function if it has shown that Latinist and vernacularist are not being stubborn about some superficial matter of pastoral practice. The whole basis of prayer, of the Church *in actu*, is at stake. It is consequently highly desirable that a few matters should be clarified. Firstly, in the *lex credendi*, some authoritative statement is needed both on the sacrifice of the Mass and on the Real Presence. Is Jesus in the Blessed Sacrament only the Way, or is he also the Truth and the Life? It is obvious that the worst possible time to reform a liturgy is when there is even the slightest element of doubt as to what it is meant to signify. Secondly, in the *lex orandi*, it is of the utmost importance that guidance should be given on two points: what constitutes the formal element of prayer, the action of the Holy Spirit or that of man; and what is the final object of prayer, the self-perfection of man or the pure adoration of God?

Until such time as these points are settled, the liturgy of the Mass proper, from the Offertory to the Communion inclusive, should not be tampered with. Indeed, it would be commendable to restore the old rite, at least permissively, in order not to prejudice the deliberations of the Fathers at Vatican III. Unfortunately, this latter would require a courage and an humility possible to a man of prayer but unlikely in a commission.

8

The Last Years at Bury

Clearly its liturgy is the most important part of any religion. It is the means of communication between God and man as well as between man and God. This is particularly true of Catholicism in which the Real Presence of God Incarnate is claimed to be made present. But the liturgy was not the only object of reform in the conciliar Church. There were plenty of others, such as married clergy, priestesses and so on. But one object of reform appeared to me particularly dangerous: the attempt to make a papal bull swallow the pill. Vernacular liturgies and the like were merely working up to the humanitarian right to contraception.

It came up officially in the fourth session of the Council, in September 1965. The outcome was certain. A great number of Catholic women started taking the pill. But the Council reserved the issue to the Holy See. The Council closed on December 8th, 1965, having gone as far as it could to disrupt the Church.

I was only an humble parish priest. I had to hear confessions for three or four hours every Saturday. "I have taken the pill three times; it seems to me alright." What am I to answer? In fact, I answered that it was all wrong. But will they believe me?

Here comes the rub. The Catholic Church claims to be of divine institution. It consequently teaches infallibly what one must believe and do for one's salvation. But for how long can what one must do for one's salvation be left in doubt? Not for a second, let alone for four years.

I gave my replies in the confessional in a second—but I had a gnawing doubt about Rome. If Rome allowed the pill, then clearly its pretensions to infallibility were nonsense. My conversion to Catholicism was an hallucination—as well as my poor attempts to holiness! I might as well commit suicide.

You see, episcopal pornography, orchestrated by Archbishop Roberts, late of Bombay, had been going on since 1962. In 1965 the Council remitted the "problem of the pill" to the Holy See. The Holy See appointed a commission to discover what was right and wrong. A leak in 1967 said that the majority of the commission was in favour of the pill. Were all my instantaneous decisions in the confessional wrong? Worse than that, over the years thousands of women must have acquired the habit of the pill. Whose fault would that be—if not that of the Church herself?

I was very depressed. The Church must be wrong, since she is incapable of giving an answer to a straightforward moral problem. But no, the Church must be right from her credentials—notably the Suffering God. What am I to do?

In early August 1968 I intended to drive up to London. I knew that my friend Edgar Hardwick, the parish priest of Coldham, wanted to go up too. I had a fast and comfortable Jaguar, so I rang up Edgar to see if he would care to come with me. He would. I went to fetch him. He was holding a newspaper. He let me drive for about twenty minutes and then asked me: "Have you seen today's paper?" "No," I replied, "I haven't taken a paper since 1954." "But I think this may interest you," and he started to read something: it was *Humanae Vitae*.

Luckily there was a layby to get off the road. I stopped the car and listened. *Humanae Vitae* was quite perfect. Edgar was a bit surprised when I hugged him and kissed him on both cheeks. "The Catholic religion is true," I cried; "one can trust the Church; salvation is real!" I drove up to London with a song in my heart. But it had been a very near thing. Could I have lasted another three months? I doubt it.

In the meantime, a curious thing had happened. The Eastern Daily Press of Norwich is one of our highly respected local newspapers. It also had a big circulation. It is owned, I believe, by nonconformists. Anyway, in 1958 I was invited to write each month an article of some six hundred words giving "the Roman Catholic point of view." I thought that such an opportunity was not to be missed. The editor was very pleased with my articles and I continued to write them up to my retirement in November 1969. That implies about a hundred and twenty articles. I still have copies of a few. They are interesting in that they give my attitude to things religious at any given time. I shall consequently inflict a few on the gentle reader, especially as they are surprisingly religious and quite often funny.

My first sample is from November 1964, and deals with the introduction of the vernacular into the Mass.

I wonder how many Catholics attend Mass on any given Sunday in England and Wales? Not far short of three million, as far as I can make out. Even in Norfolk and Suffolk, where we are notoriously thin on the ground, the figures soon mount up: over three thousand at Norwich and Ipswich, over a thousand at Bury and Yarmouth, and in numerous parishes around the five hundred. Obviously—the figures themselves prove it—we love our Mass: that incomprehensible ceremony in which the only thing we understand is the utter mystery of the True Presence of Jesus Christ under the appearance of bread and wine.

We love our Mass as it is, with its Latin mumbling, strange silences, sudden bells. Well, it is all going to be changed for us before this month is out—on November 29th. The first part of the Mass, up to and including the Creed, will be said in English.

Humans are not prone to change, and least of all in the ritual of their religion. In fact, in many religions the ritual long outlives the belief; men continue to perform the traditional acts of worship when they have long since lost any positive faith in why or what they are worshipping. So, of course, the overwhelming majority of practising Catholics in this country will be desperately sorry to see their Latin Mass go. The traditions of a thousand years and habits of a lifetime cannot be chucked overboard without the passing tear. For my own part, I rather think that the last time I cried was in 1936; I shall probably do it again on November 29th.

Of the priests I have talked to, slightly over half are in favour of the change, especially among the younger clergy who are not yet sick of the sound of their own voices. Of the many, many hundreds of laity, I have only found four individuals in favour, and they highly educated and thoroughly unrepresentative.

This is, I think, a point of some importance. The English Mass has not come about in response to any popular demand; it has been imposed by the hierarchy. It is an act of pure clericalism if ever there was one

"An act of pure clericalism": does this damn it from the start? No, and for two very good reasons.

Firstly, it proves beyond any shadow of doubt that our ritual has not outlived our beliefs: we are willing to change the one but not the other. The bishops can fiddle about with the ritual to their hearts' content, the Mass remains the Mass. Ours is no decadent religion, dependent on its outward crust to hide its inward emptiness.

Secondly, if we Catholics are willing to surrender something so obviously dear to us as the ritual of the Mass, is it not time that non-Catholics made some tiny gesture as well in this age of ecumenicity?

I shall certainly cry on November 29th. Will no non-Catholic sacrifice something and cry with me?

My second example is taken from April 1966. It illustrates the fact that I did not spare the yokels of East Anglia from sound theology.

Commercialism has succeeded in paganising Christmas and Easter: the frightful greetings cards, the yule logs, Easter eggs and all the trash—but it seems beyond the ingenuity even of blasphemy to commercialise Good Friday, when God humbled himself to an obedience which brought him to death, death on a Cross. "Father forgive them; they know not what they do." That is the trouble with us human beings: we know so little about what we are doing, but it doesn't prevent our doing it.

On the face of it, the Crucifixion ought to be the guarantee of universal damnation. It is true that most of our sins seem desperately insignificant, no matter how conceited, selfish and mean we may be; but that is largely a matter of circumstance. I am unlikely to commit a sin of cosmic significance because I am a tiny creature, acting a minute part on a very restricted stage. Given the opportunity, I could do considerably worse.

That is precisely what God has done. He has given the opportunity and, with our usual thoughtlessness, we have grasped at it with both hands, to commit the most inconceivable, impossible of crimes: deicide, the killing of God. Neither let it be imagined that so fantastic a drama is beyond the range of normal human activity. If deprived of the opportunity of killing Christ on the Cross, people will have little compunction at killing him in their hearts. They do it all around us! "Father, forgive them; they know not what they do"—although it is to be hoped that this Good Friday many will have the grace to find out.

Then, think of the Last Supper. Before dying, Christ makes his will and leaves quite precisely his body and blood as the memorial of his death. Yes, the Cross is the symbol, and the Blessed Sacrament the reality, of the greatest of all possible crimes. One would expect them to be the terrible monuments of God's impending vengeance.

Of course, they are nothing of the sort. God does not happen to work like that. All things, even evil, he shapes to a good end. The greatest of all possible crimes becomes the means of the greatest of all possible goods; the memorial of his death becomes the guarantee of our salvation.

It would be difficult to find a remark more idiotic than Voltaire's: "God has made man in his own image, and man has returned him the compliment." So little is Christianity a man-made religion that its central belief, the redemption of mankind by the assassination of God, would be inconceivable were it other than true.

God humbled himself "to an obedience which brought him to death, death on a Cross." He could not have died any other way. There is a splendid passage in Webster's *Duchess of Malfi*:

> What would it pleasure me to have my throat
> Cut with diamonds? Or to be smothered
> With cassia? Or to be shot to death with pearls?
> I know death hath then thousand several doors
> For men to take their exits.

Yes, but only one form of exit is conceivable for God Incarnate. Can one think of His being electrocuted, hanged, garrotted, guillotined? It is impossible! How inevitable is the Cross with, quite literally, the broken heart and the hands outstretched to save!

My third example comes from December 1967. What really amuses me about these articles is that they were all read by serious non-conformists and devout Anglicans. This I know because I had quite a lot of correspondence from them. Anyway, the present article is about change—and further changes in the Mass.

Life, we are told, was tough in the Middle Ages. But apparently people did not think it tough enough. Our ancestors were gluttons for penance. They thought nothing of hopping off to the Holy Land, to Rome or to Compostela with peas in their boots and instead of a toothbrush a handy little flail to whip themselves along with. As the standard of living has risen, so has penance declined, until today nobody in his senses practises any penance at all.

The Church, however, still proclaims two penitential seasons: Advent before Christmas and Lent before Easter, the former of which has just begun. Well, if Catholics simply won't practice voluntary penance, God will see to it that they practise compulsory penance. That is why our bishops introduced the vernacular liturgy in Advent 1964, and have followed it up with the Canon of the Mass in English in Advent 1967. It is a penitential exercise of the highest order, which makes peas in the boots to Compostela fade into insignificance.

The ostensible reason for it is that we live in an age of unprecedented change, so even the Mass must change every few months. We shall get some more changes next Lent, of course, and—wait for it—no, you have guessed it straight away: we shall even have a mini-Mass for youth!

Of course things change. Who has ever doubted it? Only last week I came across a photo of myself at the age of two-and-a-half months, a nice podgy baby with my mouth wide open looking for milk in the bed clothes. Doubtless, at the time, admiring aunts exclaimed: "And he's so like his father!" Yes, but he is certainly nothing like me now. I've changed. The natural process of evolution has been succeeded by the inevitable process of devolution. Incidentally, I wish scientists, or rather scientific philosophers, would include "devolution" in their vocabulary; it might help them to appear a trifle less naive.

Anyway, it is not the change that is interesting. What is so extraordinary is the underlying reality which has not changed at all. That podgy baby, that's me! Not one cell in my body, not one thought in my mind is the same; yet there is a constant factor underlying every change. It is still I, and will be to my last breath and beyond. That is extraordinary. That is worthy of intelligent consideration, rather than the claptrap about change and progress.

Objectively, it is not quite true that this age is changing more rapidly than any other, for the very simple reason that people are living longer. The human personnel—the only thing that counts—is being renewed less rapidly. Earl Russell, for instance, has been the pacifists' Chief Scout ever since I can remember. As for progress, the difficulty is to determine whether we are going down the drain or up the spout.

However, it is not change which matters, but the underlying realities. As far as the Mass is concerned, in spite of all the claptrap, God continues to utter no more than the Word made Flesh, and the faithful can give no more than their disinterested adoration.

My last article is my farewell in November 1969. It speaks—or cries—for itself.

Unwanted Priest

It has been great fun over the last ten years producing these little notes. They are not as easy as they look to write. I only hope they are easier to read. Anyway, this is the last one.

A fair amount of publicity has been given to the fact that I am resigning my parish before Sunday, November 30th, when the new liturgy of the Mass becomes obligatory. Alas, it is true.

Of course, the Mass remains exactly the same no matter what priest and people do, because God, not they, is the principal Actor. Jesus Christ still becomes present and offers himself to the eternal Father whether we stand to sing hymns or kneel in silent adoration.

But the divine action is clothed in a ceremony for which the Pope has a perfect right to legislate. Of course, he may legislate foolishly, as, it is claimed, has been done over the past thousand years and more, by providing an incomprehensible Latin liturgy. But the liturgy it was, and one had no right to use another, as indeed the reformers of today, one and all, once celebrated the old Mass.

There is a sphere, however, in which you and I are competent: our reaction to the divine action. You may be bullied and bludgeoned from pulpit or altar, but, in the last resort, you adore in your heart as you alone are able.

That is where the trouble comes. As a priest, I am obliged to function as Holy Church requires me to function. Nothing would induce me to function otherwise. But, as a simple Christian with my own soul to save, it so happens that I do not pray in the sort of way which the new liturgy implies.

Very well, the only honourable thing to do is to cease to function. If I proclaim the new liturgy with becoming fervour, I shall be a hypocrite; if I continue with the old, I shall be dishonourable. I have no intention of being either.

There it is. I go, of course, as a perfectly loyal priest and with my bishop's blessing. That is the odd circumstance of the case. When rather more priests than usual are disappearing from circulation because they are disobedient and have broken their vows, this particular specimen is going because he is obedient and has no intention whatsoever of breaking his vows. He may be a stick-in-the-mud, but he won't go down the drain.

Curious, isn't it?

Ever since the opening of the Council these little articles had presented a certain difficulty to write. On the one hand, I had to maintain what I believed: that the Catholic Church was the one, true Church, founded by Jesus Christ, infallible and indefectible. On the other hand, its liturgy and discipline were changing every few months. Moreover, the *periti* (experts) proclaimed that since its inception towards the end of the third century (!) the Church had not understood anything correctly. It was their fortuitous birth in the twentieth century and their providential meeting together at Vatican II which had laid the foundation for an intelligible Christianity. This I did not believe.

However, I think I managed to keep the Catholic flag flying during those eight years, from 1962 to 1969 inclusive. I never approved a change, but neither did I attack authority. But it was difficult.

9

I Retire

Only eight months after *Humanae Vitae*, on April 3rd, 1969, the Constitution of the new Roman Missal was published. It simply abolished the Mass and substituted—to start with—four masslets.

One extraordinary point about all this tinkering with the Mass is that the priest has gained his liberty whereas the laity have lost theirs. With the old Mass, the priest had to observe the rubrics absolutely—but the laity could do as they liked: follow the Mass in a missalette; read *The Garden of the Soul*; say the Rosary; go to sleep, etc. Now, the priest is at liberty to invent what he likes, but woe betide the laity who fail to participate. But there is a further point. The laity are still obliged to attend Mass on Sundays. But the Mass no longer exists in the Latin rite. There are practically as many Masses as there are priests. Are the laity obliged to put up with the whim of the celebrant? If so, it is grossly unfair.

Anyway, the new Mass was to come into force on the first Sunday of Advent, 1969. I wrote immediately to the bishop. Since the Canon had been altered, he had my resignation in my file since 1964. I should retire at midnight between Saturday and Sunday 29th/30th November, 1969.

Actually, on October 20th dear old Cardinal Lercaro's Commission issued an instruction saying that the old Mass could only be said by: a. retired priests; b. aged priests; c. *sine populo*—with nobody present. And the wretched laity were not considered at all. Actually, I was about to retire. Although only fifty-eight, I was sufficiently "gaga" to wish to say the "old Mass." As for nobody present, even Lercaro's Commission could not prevent Jesus Christ—who is certainly somebody—from being present at Mass, so that this restriction is *ultra vires*.

Has anybody ever read anything more uncharitable than Cardinal Lercaro's little Instruction? Is there nobody to suggest to cardinals and bishops that a tiny bit of charity might revivify the Church? And this Instruction is still the law among most bishops of Holy Mother Church.

Incidentally, we had changed bishops in the meantime. The highly competent but disagreeable +Leo had given place to the highly agreeable but incompetent +Charles in the spring of 1967. Before he left, in December 1966, I met +Leo at some clergy gathering. We were left alone—as everyone avoided him—and I took him by the lapels of his jacket and shook him: "Good heavens, my Lord! I have known you for twenty-five years. You don't agree with what is going on! Why don't you have the courage of your convictions?" He looked away and said nothing. He retired in January 1967. Poor man! He had no personal friends. His life was Holy Mother Church. She had let him down. Poor man!

Actually, 1969, the year of my retirement, was particularly busy. November 20th of that year was the one-thousand-one-hundredth anniversary of the martyrdom of Saint Edmund, which was going to be celebrated at Bury St Edmunds in a big way in 1970. I was asked to write the official Life. This I managed to do, and sent it off to the publishers before I left Bury on November 29th, 1969. To be dead honest, I did not write most of the book but dictated it off notes. It is in fact a spoken, not a written, work. This makes it particularly lively and readable. There is nothing "learned" about it, although quite a lot of learning went into it. The editors, Terence Dalton, Lavenham, Suffolk, have produced the book particularly well with many illustrations. Of course, it was not reviewed in any Catholic paper, as I had retired because of the old Mass before its publication. I had also written somewhere in the book that vandalism was not a prerogative of the barbarians since, in the twentieth century the greatest cultural heritage of the world, the Latin Mass, had been jettisoned with the fatuous flippancy of fools.

Incidentally, my delving into the story of Saint Edmund convinced me of the authenticity of his relics preserved in the splendid basilica of Saint Sernin at Toulouse. Louis, son of Philip-Augustus, the future Louis VIII, got hold of the relics when Bury

102

was sacked in July 1217. He eventually left them at Saint Sernin when he failed to carry the city of Toulouse and risked being captured by Raymond VII. He retreated from the "borough" (to the west of the city) leaving pack and baggage—including the relics of Saint Edmund and of Saint Gilbert of Sempringham. I consequently wrote to Archbishop Garrone of Toulouse, who was not yet a cardinal, asking for a relic for Saint Edmund's church at Bury St Edmunds. With the utmost kindness he let me have three loose teeth from the upper jaw. These I brought back triumphantly to my parish. On Saint Edmund's feast, November 20th, 1969, and on the Sunday within the octave, the relics were duly exposed and the faithful kissed the reliquary.

Of course, as soon as I left on November 29th, 1969, all this was abandoned. For a few years the reliquary was even lost. When it was refound, however, I decided that since Saint Edmund's parish did not want the relics I had better try the Benedictine abbey of Saint Edmund at Douai in Berkshire. I brought them there in November 1988. I have not had an acknowledgement from Father Abbot. Perhaps he had better send them back to Toulouse.

Anyway, I had to retire. One cannot retire in the abstract. One has to have somewhere to place the body. It would be impossible to retire in England because I should constantly be quarrelling with bishops, clergy, reformers, traditionalists—with everybody. No, I would have to retire abroad where everybody knows that the English are all mentally handicapped and should consequently be treated with kindness.

I was offered a splendid residence in Tuscany—but it was very remote. No, I am English and must be able to get back to my native land from time to time. On the other hand, it would be absurd not to retire to the South. What I wanted was the northern limit of the South. But how can you tell that the South has started? Ah, that's easy: the olive tree. Thus, I drove down the right bank of the Rhône until I saw an olive tree. There was a rather rickety one at Lafarge. I stopped at the next village, which is called Viviers. I had a banker's cheque with me, and bought a house in the Grand'Rue that afternoon. For sheer rapidity, the *notaire* had never seen anything like it.

The building in the Grand'Rue was a fine old house: basically fifteenth century but restored in the eighteenth. I restored it thoroughly: a new roof, oil central heating, bathroom, water-softener and the rest. But, I must admit, the Grand'Rue was a bit slummy. I could hear which neighbour beat his wife before going to bed. This did not worry me. After all, my life was finished; I was useless; I could not even be a bloody priest! So a slum rather suited me. Besides, I knew that my English friends would not mind where I lived—largely out of ignorance; whereas I did not think that my French friends would bother to keep up with me, now that I could no longer find homes in which their children could learn English. But I must admit that I grossly misjudged the French. They were wonderfully loyal. They all turned up at Viviers. They were only a bit surprised to discover that I was living in a slum. Madame de B.-J. had never been in such a street in her life; she ran back to the car park to get her chauffeur to accompany her to my house. It is really for their sake that a year later I bought my splendid residence in the "château."

Viviers is a lovely little town of about three thousand six hundred inhabitants, including the suburbs. It was the capital of the Vivarais, a province of the Holy Roman Empire up to about 1306, when it surrendered to France. It has, perhaps, the oldest ghetto in France, since Jews were not permitted in France whereas they were in the Empire. When the Vivarais joined France, one of the conditions was that the ghetto should remain. The street is now called the *Rue de la Chèverie*—which is probably a corruption of *de la Juiverie*! Anyway, it contains a lot of thirteenth-century houses.

The bulk of the town finds itself in the rather dilapidated condition in which it was at the end of the Wars of Religion in the late sixteenth century, from which it suffered much. However, there are some splendid eighteenth-century monuments, thanks to the activity of Jean-Baptiste Franque, the great Avignonese architect. It must be remembered that Avignon was the Papal States and had all the accoutrements of a minor capital. Viviers was the seat of a bishopric. The bishop's palace, by Franque, is now the town hall, but the bishop lives in the smaller but even lovelier Hotel de Roqueplane, also by Franque. Both of these buildings are on the same level as the old town. Sharply above the old town rises the "château." At present it contains the cathedral and the campanile, sixteen ancient houses, a hideous modern convent and a magnificent terrace on which stood the defensive castle until severely damaged during the Wars of Religion and finally destroyed by Cardinal de Richelieu. Incidentally, I am always surprised at the great admiration which the French have for Cardinal de Richelieu. After all, he probably destroyed more of the heritage of France than did the Wars of Religion. He was also directly responsible for the creation of Prussia—for which the French have paid fairly dearly in 1870, 1914 and 1939. However, we all know that the French are a logical race—and one only admires that for which one has to pay dearly!

But I am no longer alone in my splendid house in the château. Two doors away from me, my cousin and dear friend Geoffrey Houghton-Brown bought a house, which he has sold to his niece. The Talhouëts have bought a house the other side of the square. The Comtesse Roland is the eldest daughter of my adolescent friend, Philippe de Cossé-Brissac. Directly below the Talhouëts, my dear friend Judge Sheerin has bought a house. Thus, in my retirement, I am surrounded by friends—but when I arrived at Viviers I had none. Besides, having lived here for twenty years, I have acquired some very good French friends, people of great charm and culture.

As soon as I arrived at Viviers I called on the Bishop. I found him a man with a great deal of personality, quick-witted, intelligent and charming. He would in fact be the perfect bishop if only he had a bit of religion. By this I mean theocentricity—piety. He is totally anthropocentric and progressive. He has been bishop of Viviers for over twenty-five years, since 1964. In the 1950s the bishops of Viviers used to ordain some twenty priests each year: ten for their own diocese and ten for others and religious orders. When he came here he must still have been ordaining ten a year for the diocese. I believe that in 1970 he ordained none, which was the first time this had happened since 1792. Since then it is a common occurrence. At the moment there are two seminarians in senior seminaries, one of whom will certainly fail to go through. The situation is absolutely tragic. Incidentally, on the north side of the town stands an enormous building: the major seminary. It was built in about 1770 for three hundred students plus staff. It still had some twenty students when I came in 1969. It is now let out to anyone who needs a large building for a week or so: companies giving refresher courses for employees, the Protestant Synod, and Muslim get-togethers—what you will.

I have said that in the upper town, the château, there stands the cathedral. Even in the Middle Ages Viviers was a fairly small town, so the cathedral is not vast. In the twelfth century it had been a conventional Romanesque building with nave and side aisles. In about 1500 the choir was rebuilt in the form of one vast apse without side aisles. It is in flamboyant Gothic with Renaissance details and has spectacular groined vaulting. In the sixteenth century, during the Wars of Religion, the nave was partly destroyed. After the Wars were over there was no money to repair it, so the cathedral was left with a wooden roof over a much lowered nave and side aisles. At last, in the eighteenth century, there was the money—and the man—to do something. Inevitably J.-B. Franque was invited to restore the nave. He did so by cutting out the side aisles, thus making the nave the same width as the choir, and supporting the roof with three splendid triumphal arches. The effect is very fine: the three great arches leading up to a flamboyant ballroom. The choir has good stalls surrounding a magnificent high altar. The original lower half of this is in inlaid marble and bears every sign of being Savona work, but an archivist assures me that it was paid for at Marseille. I can only suppose that a Marseille contractor employed Savona workmen. It is a beautiful thing, and I say Mass on it every weekday.

When I came to Viviers in 1969 there was still a chapter at the cathedral and the canons said Office before the capitular Mass and a part after it. Everybody, including the bishop, was terrified of the dean, an old boy of ninety-two called Chaussinand, who was looked after by his sister aged ninety-six. The bishop gave me permission to say a private Mass in the cathedral—provided, of course, that the dean acquiesced. I consequently approached the dean with my most ingratiating smile to get the keys of the sacristy. "Of course I shall not give you the keys! I don't know you from Adam. Even if you are a priest, it does not prevent you from being a rogue and a thief. If you want to say Mass, you will have to use the high altar, as that swine of a bishop has removed all the

106

others—without the chapter's permission—except for that in the Lady chapel for the capitular Mass. You must arrive sharp at 7.45 a.m. when I open the sacristy. You must be out by 9.00 a.m. when I close it." I was duly deferential to so dominant a character.

Anyway, on July 18th, 1970, I duly said Mass in white vestments in honour of Saint Camillus de Lellis, according to the old Ordo. I was unvesting in the sacristy when the dean made his appearance. "Why have you been wearing white vestments?," he asked; "don't you know that they should be green?"

"No," I replied, "I have been saying the Mass of Saint Camillus."

"What! You were saying the Mass of Saint Camillus? You are a devout and honest man. Here are the keys to the sacristy. You can say Mass when you like. I am Camille Chaussinand!" Now, if that was not providential I should like to know what is.

The dean died a few months later. The bishop promptly suppressed the chapter. On weekdays I am, consequently, the only priest to say Mass in the cathedral. As I do so, I cannot help thinking of the piety of ages which has allowed me to celebrate the Sacred Mysteries in such glorious surroundings. Anyway, there is one cathedral in France where none but the old Mass is said every day.

10

My Congregation

Of course nobody turned up to my weekday Mass in the cathedral. Indeed officially no Mass was said at all in the cathedral on weekdays. A church in the lower town was used. On Sundays I was asked to say Mass much too early to expect a congregation. Besides, it had been announced from the pulpit that the bishop had given me permission to say Mass but no parishioner had the right to attend it. Furthermore, I knew nobody and did not want to know anybody. As far as I was concerned, my life was ended. How, then, did people get to know that there was a priest in Viviers who said the old Mass?

It was entirely providential—albeit a sad decree of Providence for me. I had scarcely arrived in Viviers when, in the spring of 1970, my good friend Paul Ghali died. He was in his early sixties; it was perfectly unexpected. I had known him intimately at Oxford when he was at Magdalen. I had met his father, Ghali Pasha, when I was in Egypt with my father, who used to maintain that he was the straightest man in Egypt. He was the Egyptian representative on the Treaty Tribunal, which determined the meaning of the clauses of the treaty of independence between England and Egypt. He had married a French woman, Baroncelli, one of the great families of the Avignonese area. Paul had consequently inherited the medieval château of Novezan as well as a fine house in Avignon. Incidentally, Ghali Pasha was the hereditary chief of the Catholic Copts in Egypt.

Anyway, Paul died. He was to be buried in Saint Agricola at Avignon. At Viviers I was almost on the spot. His very sweet widow—alas, there were no children—asked me to bury him. I drove down early to Avignon and had the facing altar and all the fun-fare removed from the church. I gave my friend a solemn Requiem.

There were a great many people at his funeral. His widow introduced me to one Madame Gabrielle Vallette-Viallard. This was a remarkable woman. She was the only daughter of a rich Protestant banking family of Nîmes. She was thus immensely rich. She was the widow of a wealthy cement tycoon, who could at least add shillings to her pounds. She was, perhaps, the last "great hostess" that France can boast. For five days a week there were only sixteen places laid for lunch, but for at least four days there were a good twenty. "But, reverend Sir," you say, "that gives nine days a week." "My dear Sir, shut up!" Anyway, she was colossal! I had scarcely met her when she said: "Monsieur l'Abbé, you have fallen directly from heaven!" "This," I replied, with my usual humility, "is perhaps an exaggeration." "Not in the least! The widowed admiral who lived at La Batie Roland died three weeks ago—and you arrive immediately afterwards. You are sent from heaven."

Now Madame Vallette-Viallard was not only the great hostess, but she also had a soul. She was a "mere marriage convert"—the type at which so many clerics jeer. She was very conscious of having changed her religion once, and she was not going to change it again. She could not stand the new Mass, which forcefully reminded her of what she had rejected. She organised my Masses for me—at least in part.

France is full of châteaux with private chapels, most of which are large and stand independently from the main building, so that tenants and neighbours could go to Mass. Also, there are a number of private churches which were bought up at the Revolution to prevent their destruction. Madam Vallette-Viallard soon organized a tour: one Sunday each month for each church or chapel.

This trudging around was excellent in theory but less so in practice. Everybody forgets where they are meant to be on any given Sunday. I decided that a central Mass at Montélimar would be preferable. Now it so happened that the Marquise de La Bruyère owned a little church in Montélimar called Notre Dame de la Rose, i.e., the *Rosa Mystica*. It is a twelfth-century leper-chapel which the Bruyères had bought up during the Revolution to prevent its destruction. I offered to buy it off the Marquise. She was perfectly agreeable, and the papers had got as far as the *notaire*. But there was immediately a howl from the religious and civil authorities. The bishop would not permit the transfer of consecrated ground to a person who said the old Mass! The socialist mayor objected that the historic heritage of France should pass out of French hands! The Marquise said to me quite simply: "As a widow, I have quite enough trouble looking after the La Bruyère estates without having the bishop of Valence and the mayor of Montélimar to contend with. You can have the church if you like, but it must remain my property." "But my dear Marquise," I objected, "the building needs at least one hundred and fifty to two hundred thousand francs (fifteen to twenty thousand pounds) spent on it to restore the roof and the ground soakaways. Had you sold to me, I should have done the lot. You could have given me a donation towards the maintenance of the tombs of your husband and his family—all buried in the church. But I am certainly unwilling to spend fifteen to twenty thousand pounds on a building which does not belong to me." I had paid her a deposit, which she returned to me.

The church is an interesting building. As I have said it is a twelfth-century leper-chapel outside the ancient walls of Montélimar. I wrote to the *Sauvegarde des Monuments Anciens*. By great good fortune, the chairman, General de Cossé-Brissac, is the uncle of the Comtesse de Talhouët. I had a wonderful reply. The *Sauvegarde* had examined the estimate of the restorers, which seemed to them reasonable: it amounted to a hundred and sixty thousand francs (sixteen thousand pounds). Provided the Marquise, as owner, subscribed forty thousand francs, and I, as user, subscribed twenty thousand francs, the *Sauvegarde* would provide the remaining hundred thousand francs. All honour to the Marquise! She paid up her four thousand pounds without a qualm. After all, she gets nothing out of it. It is I who do! The church has not been redecorated, but it is weatherproof and the soil is drained. There, since February 1984, I celebrate Mass every Sunday at eleven o'clock.

I must admit to being quite astonished at the way divine Providence has arranged things for me. Here I am, a complete failure

as a priest, incapable of being a curate or convent chaplain—
absolutely useless, in fact. But my set-up is no different from
what it would have been had I been a colossal success. I live in a
beautiful house not a hundred yards from a cathedral where I say
Mass on weekdays on the high altar. On Sundays I say Mass in a
primitive Romanesque church just about big enough to contain
my congregation of over eighty. Clearly in the eyes of God success or failure are much the same thing.

I suspect that the kindness of the local bishops is due to
Charles Grant, the charming bishop of Northampton. He passed
through Viviers on his way to Rome in 1970 and spent a couple
of nights with me in the Grand'Rue. He had lunch with Jean Her-
mil, the local bishop. What he said I know not, but it must have
been particularly flattering, as I have had nothing but courtesy
from the bishop of Viviers ever since.

11

The Fight Begins

Obviously, from the first alarm over the "adjournment"[1] of the Church and the loss of the Mass, I took up what arms I could. My dear friend and cousin, Geoffrey Houghton-Brown, was co-founder of the Latin Mass Society. At its first public meeting on April 24th, 1965 I was the only priest on the platform. I even said some perfectly sensible things: "The use of the vernacular implies domination by the clergy rather than participation by the laity... One is supposed to adore at least at weekday Masses; they are not meant to teach... It is absurd that in the presence of the Word of God we should have to listen to the words of priests... Saying is not praying... These reforms have come from clergy with no pastoral experience; they are all university or seminary professors..." I read my paper "Prayer, Grace and the Liturgy" from time to time and preached sermons where invited. But it was only after my retirement in November 1969 upon the promulgation of the Novus Ordo that I got really involved.

My retirement was reported in every newspaper and I appeared on most televisions. The consequent correspondence was enormous—most of it abusive. I suspect that it was not spontaneous but arranged by some progressive society. I wish I had preserved a few examples of it so as to entertain the gentle reader. I remember that several suggested that my retirement merely covered up my intention to marry. This I found particularly funny, as two of my ex-curates had indeed got married—and one of them, with a dispensation, in church! He even invited me

---

1 This must be a play on the word *aggiornamento* or "updating," a favorite slogan bandied about during the time of the Second Vatican Council.

to the wedding. I fear that I answered him rather sharply: "You, my dear C., are in order with the Church, although you have broken all your vows. I shall shortly be out of order with the Church precisely because I shall have broken none."

Of course I had scarcely arrived at Viviers when Paul VI canonised the forty English Martyrs, the first of whom was Saint John Houghton. I wrote a beautiful poem for the occasion. Unfortunately it was not sung, as I had intended, in Saint Peter's—but it was in many churches in England, including Saint James's, Spanish Place, in London.

Hymn for the English Martyrs

(To be sung to the tune of "The Church's One Foundation" or "I'll Sing a Hymn to Mary")

1. The Church's transformation
       By Paul VI our Pope
Has left for contemplation
       A void deprived of Hope,
Where charity is wanting
       And faith is fled as well.
One hears above the chanting
       A little hiss from hell.

2. The priest is now our ruler
       Or "president" they say.
He uses vērnacūlar
       To teach us not to pray.
He has a facing altar
       To regiment his band
And, should our voices falter,
       A microphone to hand.

3. The heretics we kiss all
       With œcumenic heart;
Alone the Roman Missal
       Had driven us apart.
To prove sincere our greetings

You see what's come to pass:
   With Eucharistic Meetings
      We substitute the Mass.

4. Hypocrisy is, clearly,
      On this the Martyrs' Feast,
   A quality loved dearly
      By almost ev'ry priest.
   The same applies to bishops
      Whose greasy statements smell
   More like our chip and fish'ops
      Than nodding asphodel.
            Ah, men! O, God!

The canonisation of the English Martyrs was the excuse for Cardinal Heenan to get the famous "English indult" for the Tridentine Mass in England. For any special occasions—marriages, funerals, pilgrimages, anniversaries, etc.—the old Mass was allowed, provided the local bishop gave his permission. This was perfectly alright for the first few years, up to say 1976, when one had a majority of old bishops, themselves used to the Tridentine Mass. But it was obvious that the Apostolic delegates would only recommend as bishops those who were against the indult. Moreover, there was a real attempt by Rome to phase out the English indult, of which more hereafter.

What a wonderful thing it is that, under divine Providence, it should have been Protestant England which saved the immemorial Mass! Not Italy, Spain or Austria, but poor little England. For twenty years she has been the only country where the immemorial Mass has been perfectly licit. Had it not been for England it would have been completely obsolete and its revival almost impossible. No, the immemorial Mass has always been licit in the Church, even if only in England.

The two chairmen of the Latin Mass Society in the early years, Geoffrey Houghton-Brown and Alfred Marnau, used to consult me from time to time. I consequently have copies of some very interesting letters. Among these are two from Archbishop Innocenti (later cardinal), then secretary of the Congregation for the

115

Sacraments and Public [*recte*: Divine] Worship, dated January 26th and May 11th, 1976.

Archbishop Innocenti relies basically on two arguments. The first and most important one is prominent in both letters. He writes on January 26th: "The title of your society is clearly linked with its origins, namely the preservation of Latin in the Church's liturgy. This is certainly compatible with acceptance of the Roman Missal of Paul VI, at present in use throughout the world, provided Latin is not understood in a way that would exclude the celebration of the liturgy in the vernacular." The same argument appears in the letter of May 11th: "The use of the Latin together with the vernacular is quite possible using the order of Mass as given in the Roman Missal of Pope Paul VI."

It seems to me highly amusing how the arguments in favour of the new vernacular liturgy—that it is comprehensible and participational—can be jettisoned in favour of the new Mass in Latin. Does this furnish a proof that there is something theological in the old Mass which is unpalatable to the modern mind? It seems strangely like it.

The second argument is best expressed in the letter of May 11th: "The Council of Trent sought a renewal of the Church's worship, as part of a general renewal in the Church, which would meet the needs of that time... In a similar way the Missal promulgated by Pope Paul VI was intended to meet the needs of the Church in our time." This is patently nonsense. Pius V codified the immemorial Mass by establishing the best available text. He allowed all rites over two hundred years old. He was not legislating "to meet the needs of the Church at that time" but to provide for all time a basic text for the Mass. On the other hand, Paul VI has promulgated a Missal precisely "to meet the needs of the Church in our time." It is meant to be ephemeral and, as time proceeds, inevitably a plethora of liturgical forms will be produced. There is really no reason why Mass in its permanent form and Mass in its ephemeral form should not coexist. What is completely absurd is to ban its permanent form. But Innocenti was not open to argument.

I had a certain amount of correspondence with English bishops whom I knew personally. One case is perhaps worth recording.

In January 1977 a group of traditionalists had written to a given bishop because they wished to make a little pilgrimage to a shrine in his diocese in the summer. They invoked the English indult for permission to have a Tridentine Mass. To their surprise, this was refused, on the grounds of its "being divisive." Their secretary was aware that I knew the bishop and asked me to intercede for them. This I did on February 28th, 1977, pointing out that "your Lordship's refusal is far more dangerously divisive than your permission could ever be… I should like to add a further remark. You cannot have failed to have noticed that the feeling between traditionalists and the hierarchy has so far been considerably less bitter in England than on the Continent. Why? Honour must be given where it is due: it is thanks to Heenan's indult. This gave the English traditionalists *hope*—and man is willing to put up with anything so long as he is not hopeless. Your refusal to implement the indult is far more serious than merely divisive: it shatters hope in countless hearts. Hopelessness is dangerous. It engenders bitterness, which begets hatred. Hatred is as resolute a motive of human action as is love. The hierarchy would be imprudent to encourage it."

I received a long and kind letter from the bishop on March 16th, but it maintained his refusal to allow the Tridentine Mass. However, it contained the following paragraph: "As to the indult, it has become highly ambiguous, and many doubt whether it should ever have been obtained. Be that as it may, the (episcopal) Conference has decided to phase it out—and it falls to each bishop to implement this decision as he sees pastorally right."

On March 28th I wrote back: "In your penultimate paragraph you write: 'As to the indult . . . the Conference has decided to phase it out.' I should be most grateful if you would let me know when and where this momentous decision was officially published, and also its exact wording."

He answered me on April 4th: "I think I have fallen into a trap of my own making by telling you of a confidential decision reached by the hierarchy. I can only ask your understanding here and count on your charity…"

Poor man! On April 14th I wrote a long letter, rubbing salt into the poor bishop's wounds. The general gist was: "The faithful will be confirmed in their belief that the revolution which has shattered their religion has been organised by 'confidential decisions' of the hierarchy..."

On April 22nd the bishop wrote longhand—presumably so that his secretary would not see it and there would be no copy. It was a pathetically apologetic letter. Its second paragraph reads: "I am deeply grateful for your letter. Whatever the deeper issues involved, I can at least reassure you that the Conference this week resolved to maintain the indult... I see that it is a right decision..."

At this point I did something which was absolutely wrong. Instead of being kind to the poor bishop, I wrote him another brutal letter on May 13th. The poor bishop wrote another apologetic little note on May 17th.

Anyway, the pilgrimage, which started all this off, got its Tridentine Mass alright. But I, quite rightly, lost a friend and created an enemy. One really must be kind—especially to fools.

Actually, I learned from Rome in mid-April 1977 that my bishop had not been perfectly honest with me. In September 1976 it was the Vatican authorities who deemed it possible to require of the English hierarchy that they themselves should ask for the withdrawal of the indult. To the perpetual honour of the English hierarchy, this was refused. But some compromisers, among them my bishop, suggested that the indult be phased out. How devious can one be?

Of course one could go on forever quoting correspondence. That is enough to show the extraordinary prejudice against the old Mass. I shall, however, end up with a quotation from a circular which I received in January 1990: "The Missal of Saint Pius V in 1570 was virtually identical with the first Roman Missal to be printed—in 1474—which in turn closely followed the Missal brought out at the time of Innocent III who died in 1216. However, the task of reforming the Mass to the primitive norms of the holy Fathers could only be done on the basis of manuscripts available to the commission under Pope Pius V. These took them back only to the twelfth century. The experts had not yet unearthed earlier books, documents, and scrolls which in later centuries were to become the study material of scholars probing the development of the liturgy of the Mass from earliest times. The Tridentine scholars thought their Mass was in fact the primitive form of the holy Fathers..."

Well I'm blowed! So the Renaissance scholars had never heard of Paschasius Radbertus, Ratramnus and Rabanus Maurus? Monastic libraries were bulging with manuscripts copied in the great scriptoria of the eighth to tenth centuries, during the Carolingian revival, but the Renaissance experts knew nothing about them? I have never heard such piffle!

The fact of the matter is that Saint Pius V wanted to establish the best traditional text of the Mass. He was even prepared to allow any discordant tradition over two hundred years old. The experts of Paul VI wanted to practice Christian archaeology and dig up the primeval Mass, before there ever was a liturgy! The two notions are clean contrary. "Tradition" is precisely what has survived through time. Archaeology is precisely the study of what time has destroyed.

Yes, the new Mass is a revival of the primitive Church, before there was a liturgy: the priest does what he likes and the faithful submit unquestioningly. But inevitably a liturgy will evolve and the chaotic Mass will disappear. But would not the hierarchy be well advised to allow the oldest liturgy, so as to pick up the fall-outs of the chaotic Mass?

12

A Step in
the Right Direction

It was in June 1971 that I received a strange circular from Cardinal Heenan. I knew Heenan quite well, as I had invited him twice, before he was a bishop, to read papers at the Higher Studies Conference when I was secretary.

The cardinal was certainly a bit agitated about something, as the circular contained no fewer than forty-one pages of print. On page 21 I learned the cause of his agitation: "The forthcoming Roman synod . . . could make recommendations to the Holy Father which might radically alter the idea of the priesthood in the eyes of both priests and laity." So that was the idea, was it? After altering the Mass, altering the priesthood! No wonder Heenan felt he needed a bit of support.

I answered him on six fully-typed pages of foolscap, practically paragraph by paragraph. Obviously I shall not inflict the lot on the reader, but a few paragraphs may be of interest. Heenan's pages 5 to 9 deal with "The Priestly Crisis." Here is what I wrote.

The document observes the fact (pages 7–8): "Some priests are deeply disturbed within themselves... apathy and insecurity... frustration... rejection... scorn." This is very true, but it does not arise from what the world may say about them, because it always has. It springs from how they feel about themselves: they have lost their *credibility* and know it. It is beside the point whether or not the violent changes which have taken place over the past ten years have been objectively good or bad. What is important is

121

that they have been of such a nature and introduced in such a way as to undermine the credibility of the clergy. What credence can be given to a bishop who proscribes one day what he prescribes the next, who, *exempli gratia*, having refused dispensations from mixed religion, now waives the promises and dispenses from the form? And what of the priest who at one time refused absolution to penitents using contraception but now declares the pill to be a matter of private conscience? One could go on indefinitely.

Moreover, there is no credibility without certainty. But there is no certainty. Even the present document assures us that we may have radically to alter our idea of the priesthood. The fact is that the four marks of the Church—One, Holy, Catholic and Apostolic—which, until recently, could be taken to signify Uncompromising, Heroic, Exclusive and Traditional, are now interpreted as Pluralistic, Permissive, Ecumenical, and Progressive. What *credibility* can bishop or priest command who acquiesces in such a change?...

The document also mentions the problem of celibacy. Now, the natural way by which a man rehabilitates himself, psychologically as well as physically, is with a woman. The sudden outcry for marriage among priests is the surest symptom of their wretchedness and misery. They pine for the security, the reassurance, the rehabilitation which a wife can give, now that Holy Mother Church no longer seems able to do so...

The real problems facing the Synod are: 1. How to reassert the credibility of the hierarchy itself in the eyes of the clergy and laity. 2. How to lift the morale of the clergy and re-instil in it the thirst for holiness and heroism... Neither will it boost the morale of the clergy "radically to alter the idea of the priesthood."

Heenan's third section, pages 9 to 24, deals with the existing doctrine of the priesthood. I have four paragraphs of slight criticism but end up: "However, it is probably churlish to criticise a section which lays no claim to be exhaustive. It is already much that, as far as it goes, it should appear orthodox."

122

We now come to the crux or kernel of the document: the six propositions on pages 24 and 25. A brief prologue warns us that the first four and part of the fifth proposition have been accepted by a vote of some anonymous International Theological Commission. The appeal to expert authority is sufficient to warn the reader that he is in for trouble. The six propositions stand by themselves. They are not a precis of the preceding Doctrinal Statement, which does not provide them with a context. This is what emerges from the mass of ambiguity:

1. There is no priesthood other than that of Christ, but in the Church it is "all the faithful" who are called to share in it (prop. 2).

2. An hierarchical ministry is, however, "necessary for the building up of the body of Christ" (prop. 2) and is indeed sanctioned by "the practice of the Apostles" (i.e., practice, not mission) and is said to be "wished by Christ" (prop. 1).

3. This ministry makes the ministry of Christ present "in the effective proclaiming of the gospel message, in bringing together and leading the community, in the remission of sins and also in the celebration of the Eucharist, by which in a special way the one sacrifice of Christ is made actual" (i.e., neither real nor offered) (prop. 3).

4. Nowhere is it suggested that the consecratory charism of the ministry is directed towards the Real Presence. It is directed towards the community: "The hierarchical ministry is necessary for the building up of a Body of Christ in which the Christian vocation is fulfilled" (prop. 2). Thus "the minister, as head of the community, represents Christ in the presence of the community" and his "pastoral office is ordered towards the Eucharist which consecrates all Christian living in the world" (prop. 4).

5. Any charism which might be considered necessary in the ministry (i.e., the power to consecrate the Real Presence) is in fact "complementary" to the ministry itself: there is "no opposition between the freedom of the Spirit distributing His gifts and the existence of a ministerial structure" (prop. 5).

6. The ministry is, however, irrevocable (prop 6).

Have you read all that? Well, you're heroic!

Have you skipped a bit? I don't blame you!

Anyway, what it means is clear: 1. The Apostolic succession is not required for ordination, since the ministry is conferred by the ecclesial group. 2. Ordination does not confer the specific charism to consecrate the Real Presence; this, if desired, is complementary to the ministry. 3. The priest is not a sacrificing minister who offers the merits of Christ, truly present, to the Father, but one who "in the Eucharist consecrates all Christian living in the world"—whatever that may mean.

We now have a clue as to what Cardinal Heenan meant when he assured us that propositions would be made which would "radically alter our idea of the priesthood." This "congregationalist" definition of the priesthood would validate the ministries of all such non-Catholics sects as had permanent ministers and would completely destroy the Catholic Church.

I had a very kind reply from Heenan in which he said that my remarks "will be very useful." Obviously, I was interested in the outcome of the synod and got hold of copies of the proceedings. I noticed that Cardinal Heenan spoke and quoted me twice—which was rather gratifying. But, much more important, the synod on the priesthood turned out to be the first total defeat of the progressive theologians, the *periti*. They had succeeded in introducing their definition of the Church as "the People of God" in *Lumen Gentium* at Vatican II. They had made the new liturgy mandatory and exclusive via the bishops. It is true that Paul VI had reacted against them in *Humanae Vitae* and in his *Credo of the People of God*. But the *periti* were able to nullify them thanks to the opposition of the bishops. In the synod on the priesthood for the first time the experts lost the support of the bishops. Their six propositions were turned down flat, without even a compromise solution. It was the dawn of hope. It was in the same year that Cardinal Heenan obtained the famous English indult in favour of the Tridentine Mass.

13

The Talking Church

Of course, living in a cathedral city in France, I meet quite a number of clergy. Also, of old driving through France on my holidays, I had met a great number of village priests, wherever I stopped off to say Mass. The two groups scarcely seem to me to be composed of the same people—by and large.

The old *curé*, riding round the village in his soutane on a lady's bike, with his chest heavily stained with snuff, who deprecated shaving more than twice a week, who lived in a presbytery full of books, wine bottles, junk, cats and what you will, is in outward appearance very different from the dapper, clean-shaven man, in collar and tie, beige suit and polished shoes, who emerges from his clean limousine to wish you good-morning. They may look very different, but is there the same person beneath the appearance? I really do not know—but I suspect that the old *curé* was far more pious and considerably more learned. Of course, he said his prayers and read books instead of watching television; but, even apart from that, he loved God and wished to explore the depths of his religion. His modern counterpart is extremely affable but he does not strike me as terribly pious. For instance, since the suppression of the Chapter in 1973, I have never caught a priest saying Mass or his prayers in front of the Blessed Sacrament in the cathedral. Doubtless they say Mass at home in their dining-rooms and their prayers in their study; but it is not quite the same thing. The old priests said Mass and the Rosary in church. It is the same with their learning. The old *curé* thought nothing of reading through his Saint Augustine and his Bossuet; his contemporary counterpart perhaps reads a progressive review.

As I have said, living in an episcopal city, I am surrounded by clergy: the bishop, the vicar-general, the chancellor, the *officialis*, the *vice-officialis*, the administrator, two other priests and the last surviving canon, aged ninety-six, who is determined to see the bishop out. They all go out of their way to be kind and agreeable to me. I am fond of them as men and even grateful to them; but I should not dare talk "religion" to any of them. That is a closed book. We are all Catholic priests, but we have a different religion. How pathetic!

Thus, the same problem confronted me in France as in England: what had induced the clergy to give in to the new ideas? I still believed—as I do to this day—that prayer is the basis of the problem, and that "Prayer, Grace and the Liturgy" gives the real answer. But how had the clergy been induced to give up praying—in fact, had lost the faith? It struck me fairly forcibly that it was the second time France had lost the faith: once in 1789 and once in 1969. Perhaps the same mechanism was at work. Anyway, I wrote the following article in March 1975.

In the revolution from which the Church is still suffering, there appears to me to be a matter of some interest which has received scant attention. How comes it that changes affecting every aspect of Catholic life have been introduced without raising an audible murmur from the vast host of clergy, bishops and priests alike? The phenomenon is far stranger than any political revolution or, for that matter, than at the Reformation, because the personnel has remained largely identical. The same bishop proscribes today what he prescribed yesterday. The priest whose range of sermons was limited to confession and company-keeping now conducts penitential services with general absolution and turns a blind eye to *Humanae Vitae*. Most astonishing of all, the holy Mass, for which every one of them would have died at the stake, has been jettisoned in the only form known to them and their flock without blush or wince. Moreover, not only was each change received without any opposition but, until quite recently, with a fair measure of applause.

That is the problem. Is one to believe that all the bishops and

126

the overwhelming majority of priests are as unprincipled as their actions are inconsistent? Such a supposition is obviously absurd. What, then, has been the mechanism which has enabled them to make such a complete *volte-face* and keep their self-respect? By what process have they swallowed dishfuls of their own words without showing any visible sign of indigestion?

It was Rousseau, a great *habitué* of Masonic Lodges and *Sociétés de Pensée*, who in his *Social Contract* first drew attention to the fact that in any discussion group, intellectual association, philosophical, political or religious club, the *volunté générale* or "collective will" was not the same as the *volunté de tous* or sum of "individual wills"; indeed, the two might be clean contrary. As Augustin Cochin pointed out in his masterly little work *Les Sociétés de Pensée et la Révolution Française*, the reason for this is not difficult to determine: a discussion group will inevitably become involved in general ideas, so that its "collective will" has as its object an abstract proposition; whereas the "individual will" always plays on given realities. Thus, it comes about that the same man may vote for "equal shares for all" but refuse a crust to a beggar. He is not inconsistent. He is in favour of the abstract idea of equal shares but is against concrete charity. He is willing to change the structures but not to practice the virtues. Incidentally, this is so true that people who constantly talk about "changing structures" can be assumed to be members of discussion groups. The "collective will," dealing as it does with general ideas, tends automatically to decide what other people should do; the "individual will," what one should do oneself.

There are, of course, certain requirements for the collective will to germinate and reach perfection. It is a hothouse plant, in need of a steady flow of hot air. The members of the group must all be considered as equal; on entering the meeting all authority must be discarded, be it of status, intelligence or experience. Specialists in a given field should be excluded or silenced when that field is under discussion; not only would they introduce prejudice, but they would be likely to embog the discussion on the technicalities of reality. The agenda should emerge from the group itself; it is not there to pass judgment on the ideas of others but to produce its own. The discussion must be open-ended and anything can be questioned; as the members are all equal, so are all opinions. Authoritative and dogmatic statements alone are to be disallowed because they are not open-ended but exclusive. It will help the group along if some of its members are endowed with instant wisdom and little knowledge; a couple of modernists will do, to provide the clap-trap. Under such conditions it is quite surprising how rapidly a few perfectly decent people can "renew the face of the earth"—far more effectively than the Holy Ghost.

Once this is pointed out it is fairly obvious, and anybody with a minimum of knowledge of discussion groups can verify the fact from his own experience.

Now, perhaps the greatest tragedy in the history of the Church occurred when the Fathers of Vatican II decided to be a pastoral discussion group rather than a dogmatic council. In matters of dogma they possessed divine authority and human competence. As a pastoral discussion group they had no more authority and less competence than the village debating society. The documents it produced are monuments to the "collective will"; they are there to be read by anyone with a sufficient supply of anti-soporifics.

Whatever one may think of Vatican II, it has had one undeniable result: it has turned the whole Church, the immaculate Spouse, the Ark of salvation, into a vast, sprawling mass of discussion groups. There are the Roman Synod, national and regional councils of bishops, the same of priests, commissions for this, commissions for that, diocesan senates, refresher courses, study days; even deanery meetings, days of recollection, retreats and in some instances the Mass itself have all been turned into discussion groups. The wretched laity have not been spared but have been dragged into commissions and councils at every level. Nobody does anything of course, because that would require an act of the individual will, but everything is discussed in an abstract, irresponsible, open-ended way. Everything is questioned, down to the foundations of religion itself. In the world of reality very little can be discussed, so hemmed in are we by circumstance, by God's divine Providence. Not so in a discussion group: at last man is free in the abstract world of his own mind, of his own irresponsible opinions. It is here that the "collective will" germinates, blossoms and fructifies.

There is a further point which should be borne in mind. The word "pastoral" has a very different meaning in the world of discussion groups and in the world of reality. The old pastoral priests used to think of their work as testifying to the dogmas of the Church by right of her divine authority. But neither authority nor dogma is allowed in a discussion group, so the word "pastoral" acquires exactly the opposite meaning: it signifies non-dogmatic and non-authoritative. When Vatican II declared itself a "pastoral" and not a dogmatic council, it did not imply that the dogmas could be taken for granted and that it wished to devise better means of imparting them to the faithful and faithless alike. What it meant was that dogmas should not be allowed to influence and prejudice the discussions at all. "Pastoral" in fact is a euphemism for "existential"; it is the adjective from "orthopraxis," since one cannot say "orthopractical." The word has deceived many good bishops and priests. Take a simple example: remarried divorcees. The old pastoral priest would talk about sanctity, heroism, living as brother and sister, or attending Mass but not going to Communion, and the like, all of which depended upon dogma. Today, however, if we are told to take a "pastoral view" of remarried divorcees we know that we are expected to abscind from all dogmatic teaching of the Church and encourage them to be daily communicants and members of the parish council.

The fact that discussion must be open-ended on the one hand and not thwarted by authority on the other leads to a curious phenomenon. The resultant collective will is permissive of any innovation no matter how outrageous, but is absolutely impatient of all tradition, no matter how desirable. This is because tradition is the most fundamental form of authority. Inevitably we witness this phenomenon all around us in the Church today, since she has become a swarming mass of discussion groups. It constitutes the revolution.

Anyone could quote a thousand examples. I shall just give one because it illustrates the matter very clearly and is taken from Roman documents. Early in 1974 the Sacred Congregations for Clergy and for Discipline of the Sacraments issued a joint statement the tenor of which was to maintain the traditional practice of the first confession before first Holy Communion. This looked much too like asserting the authority of tradition and was immediately questioned by the National Council of Canadian Bishops. Straight away the Sacred Congregations climbed down and in an addendum to their recent Catechetical Directory write: "Our declaration is not intended to impose constraint, moral or otherwise." Of course not; the Sacred Congregations saw the light through the open end. In the meantime, in October 1974 the Sacred Congregation for the Liturgy [*recte*: Divine Worship] issued a "notice" that the new Order of Mass was obligatory, "immemorial custom notwithstanding." The point of interest is not the legal value (if any) of this notice but the attitude of the Sacred Congregation. As against the permissiveness in the first case, in the second there is "every intention of imposing constraint, moral and otherwise." The reason is clear: the immemorial Mass in the old rite is the most universal, most venerable, most dogmatically exclusive and consequently most authoritative tradition in the Catholic Church. Go it must if ours is to be an open-ended religion. *Lex odiosa non est restringenda*:[1] yes, vexatious laws should not be made to bind too rigorously, except when it comes to the immemorial Mass. The shelves of the Index have been emptied of all their rubbish in order to make way for that stupendous volume, the old Roman Missal.

Indeed, precisely because of its enormity, the persecution of the old rite provides admirable examples of the conflict between the collective and individual wills. The vast majority of bishops could be labelled "decent scouts," men who are keen to please, eager to do their good deed. There is not an ounce of cruelty in their make-up. They would not swat a fly if they could avoid it. That is at the individual level. Yet collectively they are party to the most flagrant act of cruelty which the Church has ever perpe-

---

1 The author is misremembering the axiom: what he writes would mean that an odious or vexatious law should *not* be taken restrictively, i.e., as narrowly as possible, whereas the opposite is true: the old axiom is *odiosa restringenda, favorabilia amplificanda*, or, as Buontempi says, "Lex odiosa non est extendenda, quia odia sunt potius restringenda, non vero amplianda" (a vexatious law is not to be extended [to include more in its scope], because odious things are rather to be restrained, not amplified). The axiom is found in the 1983 *Code of Canon Law* as canon 18.

trated by depriving millions of the faithful of the Mass they love. The cruelties of the Wars of Religion or of the Spanish Inquisition pale into insignificance beside it; they affected vastly fewer people, cut far less deep and were infinitely less unjust. True, the few priests who cling to the Mass of their ordination are not burned at the stake. It might be better if they were, like Joan of Arc by Bishop Cauchon, probably himself as decent a scout as any.

Apart from the cruelty there is the question of hatred. The majority of bishops taken individually are incapable of sustained hatred; collectively they hound down the old rite with a bitter venom worthy of a better cause. There was scarcely a frown for the most sacrilegious Eucharistic innovations. The fact that they are illicit and the priests disobedient matters not at all. But woe betide the priest who innovates with [i.e., resumes] the old rite! Clearly, it is not the question of liceity and obedience which makes the difference; it is the Mass that counts. Like Carthage, *Missa est delenda*. There is not a bishop who wanted such a state of affairs to arise. It has not come about by the sum of their individual wills. What has happened is that in their diverse discussion groups they have generated a formula inimical to tradition; the collective will has spoken and they themselves must bow.

It would be idle to multiply examples. The point is that bishops and priests are not as unprincipled as their actions are inconsistent. They have merely allowed their individual, responsible, God-made will to be submerged by a collective, irresponsible, man-made will. It is not a good swap. This is doubtless the same in all revolutions, political and religious alike. Man is perpetually attempting to impose his own intellectual, abstract conception of order on to the reality of God's exuberant creation. Man always appears to be on the verge of success yet forever fails, as, no matter how tight the strait-jacket, reality bursts out at the seams.

Anyway, if the present auto-destruction of the Church is to be halted, the first thing to be done is to stop talking. In the ensuing silence we shall again be able to hear the still, small voice of God at Mass, and in the world the Church proclaiming the eternal truths.

It was in the following year, 1976, that I spent a couple of nights at Northampton as the guest of Bishop Charles Grant, on my way up to Hoghton Tower in Lancashire. There was a fairly large luncheon party the day after my arrival: half-a-dozen clerics and as many laymen. In the course of conversation, Charles said to me: "It is all very well for you, Bryan, to criticise me over the old Mass, but what would you actually do if you were in my position?" "My dear Charles," I answered, "I do not want to bore the assembled company with an answer but shall send you a written reply from Viviers when I get home."

I sent him the answer early in 1977. It is "The Bomb," the first chapter in my book *Mitre and Crook*, pages 11 to 19. The rest of the book is pure imagination, but not the first chapter: it is a real document sent to a bishop. When, in 1977, I stayed with him again on my way north, dear Charles merely jeered at me: "You are a joke, Bryan! I have rarely laughed so much in my life imagining bishops X and Y reading your Bomb!" Anyway, I decided to use it as the basis of a book. *Mitre and Crook* was published in America in 1979, and in France in 1982 as *La Paix de Mgr Forester*.[2]

Actually, and in spite of Charles, I find the suggestions made in the Bomb perfectly sensible. The old Mass (1962) and the new (1969) become equally licit. There are a few minor corrections to the new Mass. A hybrid Mass is also allowed: "I see no reason why the pre-Mass, up to and excluding the Offertory, should not be said in alb and stole according to the new Order and calendar, facing the people from the ambo. The celebrant will then ascend the altar, don the chasuble and celebrate the Mass itself, back to the people and in Latin, according to the immemorial rite, up to and including his own Communion. For the Communion of the faithful he could revert to the vernacular and, after purifying chalice and fingers, end the Mass according to the new ordo." There are some simple rules as to which Mass should be said. The hybrid Mass would satisfy the obligation of a progressive priest to say the old Mass, and the traditionalist to say the new.

2 The English edition was republished by Angelico Press in 2019.

Actually, I am surprised that my suggestion has not been taken up officially. It seems to me highly desirable that all priests of the Latin rite should have a Mass in common—the hybrid—as well as the Masses which differentiate them, even if both be allowed.

Incidentally, *Mitre and Crook* sold quite well. It had to be reprinted both in English and in French. The French editor sent several copies to Rome. He had a surprising reply from one cardinal: "There are passages in the book one cannot read without their bringing tears to one's eyes." So I have made a cardinal cry! That is a bit of an accomplishment, isn't it?

I also delivered several lectures on "Peace in the Church" with my hybrid solution—to a university summer school at Fanjeaux, in Paris and in Geneva. The principal opposition came from the Lefebvrists—which I well understand. They are fighting for the integrity of the Mass and of the religion, pure and unadulterated. But they forget the vast sprawling mass of desolate Catholics who have neither the liturgy nor the doctrine. How in practice is one going to try to give them back both? It is certainly not through the intransigence of a few hundred Lefebvrist priests that it is going to be done. By hook or crook one must somehow get the old Mass back—for the sake of the people, not for the sake of being right oneself.

14

The Lake of Geneva

Viviers is very well situated. It is in the South of France and consequently only an hour's run from Avignon and under two hours from Arles or Nîmes. But it is on the fringe of central France and two hours from Lyons, and under four from Geneva, even observing the speed limits. Bern is the administrative capital of Switzerland. Thanks to my friend, Claude Martingay, author and publisher, I have been invited several times to lecture at Geneva or Lucerne. I have even appeared on television in Switzerland.

Anyway, on October 20th, 1983 I delivered a full-dress lecture of one-and-a-half hours at Lucerne. I think it was interesting, but much too long to write out in full. I shall consequently translate and transcribe my fairly copious notes.

1. Introduction. In 1934 Orwell pointed out that one creates the future by falsifying the past. An excellent example in 1977: Professor Jean Delumeau's *Will Christianity Die Out?* He claims that Christianity lost the intellectuals in the seventeenth century thanks to the condemnation of Galileo; it lost cultured classes in the eighteenth; the working classes in the nineteenth; the bourgeois in the twentieth.

2. The *reality* is the extraordinary vitality of Christianity up to 1962.

    a. The French Revolution forms a watershed: before it, the leading countries were France, Austria, Spain—all Catholic; after it, the leading countries were England, Prussia, Russia—all non-Catholic.

b. However, never has Catholicism expanded so much or so rapidly:

i. I am in Switzerland—in my youth still a respectable Protestant country: J.-J. Rousseau, the Neckers, Klopstock, Nietzsche. Today Geneva, international capital of Protestantism, is in majority a Catholic town. The only internationally known Swiss are both RC: Cardinal Journet and Hans Küng!

ii. Germany, with Prussia and the *Kulturkampf* to contend with in the last century, and in this century, Hitler, produced von Galen and von Preysing. Today, the Federal Republic is majority Catholic. After the war, there was President Adenauer.

iii. Italy. It was thought that the loss of the Papal States would be the end of Catholicism. Not in the least. Rosmini, John Bosco. The definition of Infallibility. Great popes: Pius IX, Leo XIII, Pius X, XI and XII. After the war, Premier De Gasperi.

iv. In the USA, the first Catholic president, Kennedy.

v. In France, in spite of social instability—Restoration, Louis-Philippe, Second Republic, Second Empire, Commune, Third Republic, etc.—the hundred and fifty years from 1815 to 1962 are among the most glorious in its ecclesiastical history:

a. In religion, from Dom Guéranger and Lacordaire to Charles de Foucault, with the Curé d'Ars, Bernadette of Lourdes, Saint Thérèse; Cabrol, Chautard, Marmion—it is incredible!

b. In sociology: Le Play, La Tour du Pin, Albert de Mun, etc.

c. In 1905, the Combes laws—everything confiscated. Within twenty years everything rebought or rebuilt—a financial effort equivalent to medieval cathedral-building.

d. Before the Council, the best-known authors were mainly RC: Leon Bloy, Charles Péguy, Paul Claudel, Jacques Maritain, Bernanos, Mauriac, Gabriel Marcel, etc.

vi. But the vitality of pre-Conciliar Catholicism most evident in England: Emancipation in 1829: a quarter of a million Catholics, i.e., under one percent; in 1960, six million Catholics, i.e., twelve percent. Hereditary English Catholics amounted to a few ancient families and depressed industrial workers. There was no peasantry, no artisanery, no middle-class until the 1920s. The elite is composed of converts. Churchmen: Faber, Newman, Manning, Abbot Chapman, Ronnie Knox, etc. Poets: Patmore, Wilde, Hopkins, R. Campbell, Siegfried Sassoon, etc. Writers: Baring, Chesterton, Charles Dawson, Ross-Williamson, etc. Novelists: Benson, Evelyn Waugh, Graham Greene, Bruce Marshall, etc. I can only think of three famous cradle-Catholics: Belloc, one hundred percent French; Martin D'Arcy, one hundred percent Irish and Jesuit; Edward Elgar, one hundred percent musician.

vii. Apart from Europe, remember the colossal *missionary expansion*. In spite of politics, of two world wars, of the moral collapse of the West, *the Church was in full expansion*.

3. I myself am a convert, i.e., a part of the expansion.

From 1940 to 1965 I received about ten converts a year—between two and three hundred in all.

Luckily, no more converts after 1965. How could I have explained that One, Holy, Catholic, Apostolic and Roman had come to mean Pluralist, Permissive, Ecumenical, Evolutionary and Collegial?

Had I deceived my converts? Had I myself been deceived?

I was heartbroken!

4. Undeniably, the crisis starts in 1965, at the close of the Council. The statistics for England show it—although it is the country which has suffered least, thanks to Heenan's indult and English pragmatism.

a. Converts: in 1953, 12,000; in 1959, 15,800; in 1965, 10,300; in 1980, 5,401.

b. Baptisms: in 1953, 91,000; in 1964, 137,700; in 1965, 134,000; in 1980, 73,016.

c. Marriages appeared to have gone up before the fall: in 1953, 36,000; in 1968, 47,400; but in 1980, 28,545.

d. Ordinations: from 1953 to 1966 they vary from 110 to

138; in 1969, under 100; and in 1981, only 87.

Evidently, a board of directors would have reacted violently towards such statistics: fall-off of new clients—converts; heavy shrinkage of existing ones—baptisms and marriages; shortage of salesman—ordinations. The company faces bankruptcy!

5. Do the bishops realize what has happened? Yes! But they cannot beat their own breasts: they have always acted out of the *highest moral motives*. Most bishops are good but stupid men. As usual, they beat the breasts of their opponents: a. the Spirit of the Age; b. the traditionalists and that God-sent scapegoat, Monsignor Lefebvre!

6. But the collapse of empire is usually due to *internal* not *external* causes. The collapse of the French Empire was not due to what happened at Saigon, Algiers or New Caledonia, but what happened in Paris. The same with the collapse of British Empire—caused not by what happened at Delhi or Salisbury, but in London. There was an interior loss of *confidence, certitude* and *faith*.

This is precisely what has happened to our board of directors, the bishops. They have lost *confidence, certitude* and *faith*. Christ's Empire, the Church, has consequently crumbled.

Such was my lecture at Lucerne. Actually, it was quite a good lecture, although its notes do not read frightfully well. Anyway, I think it destroyed Professor Delumeau's contention that the Church was in full decline well before the Council. It may have been in certain difficulties in France, but France is not the world—in spite of what most Frenchmen seem to think!

15

An Interlude

When I had arrived and unpacked at Viviers, I learned that there was a Benedictine priest about sixty miles away who had founded a priory for the traditional Mass. I went to visit him.

The priory was beautifully situated, in the lap of Mount Ventosus (Mont Ventoux), from the summit of which Petrarch claimed (quite wrongly) to have seen the Alps, the Mediterranean and the Pyrenees. The Mediterranean was doubtless flood water near Arles, and the Pyrenees the southern range of the Cevennes. Anyway, the priory was at Bedoin, from which there was a magnificent view. The little church was very beautiful, early twelfth century, and there were a few stone buildings. The whole belonged to a family who owned a charming house less than a hundred yards down the drive.

The priory contained exactly two monks: the prior, Dom Gérard Calvet, OSB, and one postulant, Brother John. They said the whole monastic Office at each other and made the old stone buildings ship-shape. Suddenly novices began to appear—one, three, six, nine. There must have been a dozen of them by 1973. The old stone buildings were crowded out and used as refectory, parlour, library and for other community functions. The monks' cells became a row of caravans in the courtyard.

That Dom Gérard is kind, very sensible and has the most attractive personality is true, but I doubt if that is the cause of the vocations. These were due to the fact that Bedoin was the only Benedictine monastery in France which obeyed the complete Benedictine rule—including night Office—and said the old Mass. But how was Dom Gérard going to get minor orders for his novices and eventually major orders? Minor orders had been suppressed. Besides, the archbishop of Avignon took a dim view of Dom Gérard because he said the old Mass. It must be remembered that all of this took place before the retirement of Archbishop Bugnini in July 1975, at the time of the greatest hysteria against the old Mass. In fact, the only bishop willing to give his novices minor orders was Monsignor Lefebvre—still at that time in order with the Church. Dom Gérard invited him to do so. He also invited me to attend. I went without a qualm: the local bishop refused to give minor orders and Lefebvre was still in order.

When I arrived at Bedoin I had difficulty in parking because of two large buses and masses of children milling about the place. However, I managed to get into the diminutive church and found a seat reserved for me. I discovered that the two bus-loads of children had come from Marseilles in order for them to be confirmed by Archbishop Lefebvre. Obviously, each child had his proud father and mother, plus four grandparents, plus uncles and aunts.

The diminutive church could take about twenty people in the choir, including Archbishop Lefebvre, Dom Gérard and a couple of monks wiping the chrism off the kiddies' foreheads; and about fifty adults in the nave and side-aisles—provided the children came in through the only door and squeezed out of it again at the end.

Luckily, I am a fairly narrow-hipped male because I had to surrender three-quarters of my reserved chair to the mother of one of the *confirmandi*. Anyway, they all disappeared (for the moment) and we could get down to giving minor orders to the monks.

We had all to meet again at a colossal *déjeuner* at Malaucène, the local town. It was clear that a bit of time would be required to get us all eating, so I asked Lefebvre if he would come and have a whisky with me at the bar. After a bit of back-chat, I asked him if he had got permission from the bishop of Marseilles "for all those confirmations you have done?"

"Of course not! I did not even know that I should be expected to confirm. But, when all those good parents turned up, what can one do but confirm their children?"

But I suspect that he must have had a very shrewd idea that he was going to be asked to confirm.

140

"But come on, my Lord, you know that confirmation is about the only direct contact between a bishop and his flock. Surely you realise that you make yourself extremely unpopular by confirming right and left?"

"Unpopularity with bishops is the last thing that worries me. What does worry me is whether they will confirm validly."

"Do you require that your secretary notify the place of baptism of the children whom you have confirmed?"

"Of course not. Dom Gérard keeps a register and issues certificates to the parents. That is quite enough!"

I forget all the questions I asked him, and I doubtless asked them less bluntly than I have put them down here. But the fact remains that, way back in 1973, I got the impression that Lefebvre was perfectly willing to start a parallel Church.

I may say that this was not the first time that I met Monsignor Lefebvre. I had already met him (perhaps in the summer of 1969) at the Kenworthy-Browns. There had been present: Mr and Mrs Kenworthy-Brown, Monsignor Lefebvre, Mr and Mrs de Saventhem, Mr Geoffrey Houghton-Brown, Mr Vernor Miles (representing the Countess of Kinnoull) and myself. Monsignor's lack of English was a bit of a bore, but luckily the de Saventhems, Geoffrey and I were fluent in French, and the Kenworthy-Browns understood most of it, although a bit tongue-tied. But poor Vernor Miles was still at school-French: "My aunt's pen: *la plume de ma tante.*" This was perhaps rather fortunate—divine Providence. Monsignor Lefebvre wanted money to start up in England in a big way. Now, Vernor Miles represented Lady Kinnoull, who had one of the biggest Catholic fortunes in England. It had been left to her by her husband and she was childless. At the crucial moment Mr Vernor Miles was unable to understand.

Anyway, the problem was: whether the Latin Mass Society should associate itself with Lefebvre or not? It was decided that the two organisations should remain divided: the LMS trying to get the hierarchy to admit the old Mass; Lefebvre producing the old Mass in spite of the hierarchy. I felt quite sure that this was the right decision.

I got to know Monsignor Lefebvre reasonably well. I called on him at Écône in 1974. I attended a retreat he gave at Flavigny in

1975—and I met him regularly at the Prieurs' house at Richeranche, not twenty miles from Viviers. A word is necessary about the Prieurs of Richeranche. These are well-off people who own a beautiful old converted farmhouse with its private chapel. They can easily afford to put up Lefebvre and his secretary—but they are not the Comte and Comtesse de X, which might give the wrong impression. To get from Écône to southern France, be it to Marseilles and Nice or to Toulouse and Bordeaux, one has to get around the Alps. One day's drive from Écône around the Alps brings one to Richeranche. Hence Lefebvre was a fairly constant visitor at the Prieurs'. Whenever he stayed the night, there was a dinner party to which the local resistance priests were invited, including myself—especially as I am considered a sort of ecclesiastical clown who could jolly the party along. It was at one of these parties that I interrupted Lefebvre with a remark: *On ne sauve pas la foie en démolissant l'Église*—you cannot save the faith by destroying the Church. It halted Lefebvre in his stride for perhaps a minute. But Dom Gérard Calvet whispered to me a little later: "Of course you are right!"

This brings me back to Dom Gérard at Bedoin. It was clear that the owners of the property were getting a bit restless. They had imagined a few pious Benedictines chanting the Office in their little church and strolling round the grounds in deep meditation. Not a bit of it! Their drive was blocked by char-à-bancs. The property was getting covered with cell-caravans. The church was so packed by monks that they could scarcely get in themselves. So, naturally enough, they gave Dom Gérard notice. I forget what date that was—in 1976? Anyway, they allowed Dom Gérard to stay until he had found alternative accommodation.

Dom Gérard immediately thought of restoring one of the great medieval abbeys of Provence: Sénanque, Silvacane, le Thoronet or Montmajour. But, of course, neither Church nor State would allow him to have one! The narrow-mindedness and sheer stupidity of "institutions" passes belief. So, Dom Gérard decided, in the middle of the twentieth century, to build a vast Benedictine abbey in Provence. This is exactly what he has done.

He has chosen a superb site, a long mile outside the village of Le Barroux and some six miles south of the township of Malaucène. It is on top of a fairly low hill with a splendid view of Mont Ventoux to the northeast and looking out west onto the astonishing Needles of Montmirail. The abbey is built on a magnificent scale for sixty to eighty monks. Everything is complete excepting the arcades of the great cloister: all the cells, refectory, monastic kitchens, chapter house, guestrooms, parlours; the vast abbatial church, over-crypts, sacristies, a tower plus bells—one of which was given by Gustav Thibon, etc. Apropos of bells, I had an English Benedictine with me. He wandered into the church just before midday. He witnessed the ringing of the Angelus. The monks pulled the bells by hand-ropes coming through the vaulting of the choir. After the Angelus, the little "voluntary" played by the bell-ringers was simply superb. My very progressive English Benedictine friend was nearly converted to the old religion! The abbatial church, built, as I have said, over a vast crypt, to allow for private Masses, is in the usual thirteenth-century Provence style, rather like Sénanque: narrow side-aisles and wide nave; the vault slightly pointed but no groins, so that the weight of the vault comes on the walls, not on the pillars. It is austere and perfectly lovely. The church was consecrated by Cardinal Gagnon on October 2nd, 1989. He did it splendidly. The ceremony took about five hours, from 9.00 a.m. to 2.00 p.m. Not having drunk anything since 6.00 p.m. the previous night, I was able to last out.

Incidentally, when Lefebvre consecrated his bishops on June 30th, 1988, Dom Gérard did not follow him. He accepted peace with the Church on the understanding that his abbey would continue with the old rite. This was granted.

Now, I do not pretend to be well informed. I have not subscribed to a newspaper since 1954. I have never owned a wireless or television in my life. As far as I can see, there are only two pieces of information which it behoves me to know: 1. when the clock changes; 2. when war is declared. I have a friend who has promised to ring me in both eventualities. Otherwise, I rely on kind friends to give me by post their mature judgments on social, religious or political events.

After the 30th June 1988 my post must have doubled. Fifty percent of the letters were written to convince me that Dom Gérard was disloyal, a rogue and a traitor. Never have I read such scurrilous, offensive diatribes. They made me feel so grateful that, although a staunch traditionalist, I had never been associated with any of their groups. I wrote to Dom Gérard to congratulate him on having left the company of such snarling, spiteful brutes. In actual fact, Dom Gérard is among the most intelligent, cultured, kind and sensitive men I know. His sensitivity must have made him suffer much from the wanton abuse hurled at him. But he has survived, and his abbey has sixty monks.

16

Irreligion

I have got right up to 1990 with Dom Gérard Calvet, but I'm still in the early eighties as far as I myself am concerned.

In 1982 I gave two lectures on "Irreligion" to the Centre Charlier's summer school. I later fused them together, and the result was published along with another essay as a booklet in 1987 in France. It has never been published in England but, judging by the French reaction, it is worth doing. In part it is, perhaps, a bit technical, but nothing like as bad as "Grace, Prayer and the Liturgy."

I knew exactly what I wanted to say but had insufficient time between the invitation and performance to collect the apparatus usual at such lectures. Fortunately, I knew whence I could collect it: from the Gifford Lectures (1974–76) given by professor Stanley Jaki OSB and published in 1978 by the Scottish Academic Press under the title of "The Road of Science and the Ways to God." The most interesting items in the following paper, delivered on 28th November, 1982, are the quotations, most of which have been provided by Professor Jaki.

The phenomenon unique to the age in which we live is not really the computer, the television or even the atom bomb. It is that never before has irreligion, atheistic or agnostic, been taken universally for granted. In one half of the world religion is positively persecuted, and in the other ignored as irrelevant. The phenomenon is at once so obvious and so unique as to cause surprise that nobody seems to have studied it in depth. Even the organised religions—and notably the most organised, the RC—seem to take so extraordinary a situation as inevitable. We have even been asked to be "open to the world," which means in fact to irreligion. Obviously, I lack the competence to supply a study in depth; all I can do is to draw attention to the phenomenon, and to certain aspects thereof sufficiently blatant for all to see.

Ir-religion, a-theism, a-gnosticism are all negatives. Of themselves they mean exactly nothing. Their meaning depends on what is denied, on the preconceived idea one may have of religion, God and knowledge. This complicates the issue, as an atheist would clearly be right to deny his wrong idea of God; it might help him to recognise the true one. But we have gone beyond that. We have arrived at the point where, on an absolutely *a priori* judgment and against all possible evidence, there is no possibility of God's existing and therefore of knowing Him and of making significant acts towards Him.

So radical an atheism, *a priori* to all evidence, is clearly unscientific. It is epistemological. That is to say that it concerns the grounds on which we know anything, let alone God. It consequently behoves us to formulate the theist epistemology which the atheist denies. It is surprisingly simple and can be summed up as follows: i. all phenomena, including the human intelligence, are objective entities, created and governed by the divine Intelligence; ii. the human intelligence, being made in the image of God, is capable of understanding all phenomena and the laws which govern them by a process of induction or inference. The *a priori* atheist will have to deny one of those two propositions. Hence the two groups into which they naturally fall:

1. The idealists, who maintain that the human intelligence can only grasp its own ideas. It could not grasp an objective reality outside itself, even if such a reality existed. Such is the system of Descartes, Kant, Hegel and their followers.

2. The empiricists, who admit the objective reality but deny that the human intelligence can do more than grasp the phenomenon. Any induction or inference he may make has no objective value. Only that is true which can be empirically verified, i.e., by physical experiment. Such is the school of Bacon and Hume.

The fact is that to deny God on *a priori* grounds one first has to deny that man is a rational animal. It is pure agnosticism: we cannot know God because we cannot know anything. The idealist has lost his body and the empiricist his head. Both schools of thought lead eventually to an impasse: how can one know what one cannot know? Nevertheless, both have played havoc with Western thought since the Reformation.

But there are epistemological difficulties which are less radical. It is obvious that different forms of knowledge are accepted as true on different criteria. An historical is not a mathematical proof; a proof in physics is not the same as in geometry. And this quite apart from value-judgments as to what is good, beautiful and the like. One cannot help wondering sometimes whether the atheist is using the correct criteria for his subject. I agree whole-heartedly that I cannot prove the existence of God by geometry and, if I tried, I should know that I had gone mad. It seems that some atheists fail to realise this: estimable characters, doubtless, but triangles in which all angles are obtuse.

All this is by way of introduction to a very broad and difficult subject. It may also help to explain certain attitudes prior to the Incarnation which seem odd to the twentieth-century Christian.

I suppose we should all agree that in the pre-Christian West three of the greatest philosophers in their respective fields were Socrates and Aristotle in metaphysics and Cicero in ethics. Very well: Socrates, the champion of teleology (design in the universe) requested before his suicide that a cock be sacrificed to Asclepius; Aristotle, who considered God as the pure act, one and indivisible, left a substantial sum in his will to erect statues to the gods of Greek mythology, Zeus and Demeter; Cicero, who wrote the fundamental work on agnosticism, *De Natura Deorum*, was for two periods in his life the Pontifex Maximus of the Roman pantheon.

The Catholic immediately wonders whether they were in good or bad faith, but to them the question did not arise. The criteria by which they judged their religion had nothing to do with objective truth. They employed the criteria of poetry, art, sociology, but not the criteria necessary for belief. Religion was a series of acts which had to be done, not a series of dogmas which had to be believed. It was a sort of white magic when it was not a sort of black magic.

147

It is precisely the uniting of the two notions of "religion" and "truth" which is the fundamental result of the Incarnation and consequently of the basic attitude of Christians. We find it very difficult to imagine a state of affairs in which religion had no pretension to be true—although we may be edging back to it ourselves.

In this connection, several points seem worth mentioning. The pre-Christian world produced no theology but a vast mythology to which its philosophy (physical and metaphysical) was entirely alien. Christianity immediately produced a vast theology which incorporated all philosophy. The intellectual achievement of the Fathers and Doctors of the Church is an unique phenomenon in the history of mankind. It was based on the assumption that all truth served religion because religion was all-truth. Antagonism between religion, philosophy and science was inconceivable. Had not Jesus himself proclaimed: "What I came into the world for, was to bear witness to the truth" (John 18:37)?

The trouble with truth is that inevitably it is both exclusive and universal. It is truth which is "catholic" and the term is applied to Christianity merely because it claims to be true. If, however, religion is not thought of as being true, it automatically becomes tolerant and ecumenical. This, indeed, was the primary characteristic of pre-Christian religions: they were ecumenical to the point of building the Pantheon and sufficiently tolerant to erect altars to the Unknown God. The one exception was Judaism, which claimed precisely to worship the "true" God. But even it was persecuted primarily because of the exclusiveness of the race rather than because of the exclusiveness of truth—an idea incomprehensible to the pre-Christian in matters of religion. Hence the extraordinary fact that purely religious persecutions and wars of religion are post-Christian phenomena. As Jesus said: "Do not imagine that I have come to bring peace to the earth; I have come to bring a sword, not peace" (Matthew 10:34). No prophecy has ever been more clearly or more constantly fulfilled.

One last point. If religion is not considered as assent to the truth but as a series of social acts, automatically all social acts will tend to acquire a religious connotation. This is precisely what had happened in the pre-Christian world. Even the butcher supplied his customers with meat that had been sacrificed to Jupiter, Mars or Venus. And this state of affairs still exists in those parts of the world where Christianity or one of its derivatives has little influence—parts of Africa and India. Humans are perfectly willing to allow their lives to be dominated by religion provided it is false—in the sense that it lays no claim to being true. In fact, irreligion is a by-product of Christianity.

This last statement I believe to be profoundly true—to the point of being self-evident. An unshakable faith in disbelief is only to be found in what was once Christendom.

The reason is not far to seek. That God created man with freedom of choice, although not independent, automatically implied the possibility of the wrong choice, of evil—with all its consequences. That God should reveal Himself by His Incarnation automatically implied the possibility of His total rejection in atheism and irreligion.

The fundamental causes of sin and irreligion are exactly analogous. Just as the fact of sin, no matter how subjectively justified, indicates the existence of a natural law, so does atheism, no matter how intellectually justified, indicate the reality of Revelation.

So much for the rather theoretic but not least important part of the present lecture.

I doubt if since the Crucifixion of our Lord a single generation has passed without somebody writing a major work to prove, once and for all, that Christianity is rubbish. The zeal, erudition, single-mindedness, love and labour which, over two millennia, have been spent on disproving our religion must make a Christian feel ashamed. Christianity has certainly made some of its enemies practise the virtues, if not all of its adepts. The history of irreligion, with its undoubted geniuses, laborious devotees and charlatans, by its very variety might well afford the best possible vindication of what it denies.

It is all very well, however, to assault this or that Christian dogma, but sooner or later it is the first article of the creed, God the Creator, which will come under attack. This is what has happened. If science can disprove the truth of creation, the idea of God can safely be relegated to mysticism, which begins with mist and ends in schism. Thus Professor Jaki is surely right to identify the contemporary battleground as being cosmology, the nature of the universe.

Like its epistemology, Christian cosmology is basically quite simple: i. there is a personal, transcendent God, infinite and eternal, who creates all things *ex nihilo*; ii. the creation is contingent, finite and temporal; iii. but it reflects its Creator and iv. is therefore good, true, purposeful and comprehensible; v. thus it manifests its Creator by the five ways of causality, movement, contingency, perfection, and design. Such is the notion which must be disproved and denied.

It is not as easy to disprove as it looks. In the first place, an empirical scientist ought not to have a cosmology at all. The universe is not an empirical datum but an inference drawn from a host of empirical data. The moment he uses the word cosmos or universe he is philosophising and has ceased to talk scientifically. But that is only the start of the empiricist's adventure into metaphysics: having postulated the universe, he promptly applies to it the attributes of God. He is obliged to. Since there is no God, it is the universe which is self-subsisting, infinite and eternal.

Jaki (page 435) illustrates this point perfectly. It is a quotation from C.F. von Weizsäcker's *The Relevance of Science*. In 1938 von Weizsäcker, an atomic physicist, had suggested to Nernst, a Nobel laureate, that the age of the universe could be calculated on the basis of radioactive decay: "He (Nernst) said, the view that there might be an age of the universe was not science... He explained that the infinite duration of time was a basic element of all scientific thought, and that to deny this would mean to betray the very foundations of science. I was quite surprised by this idea and I ventured the objection that it was scientific to form hypotheses according to the hints given by experience, and that the idea of an age of the universe was such a hypothesis. He retorted that we could not form a scientific hypothesis which contradicted the very foundations of science." Well, there it is. Unlike a host of lesser scientists, Nernst was willing to admit that infinite duration was not a scientific inference but an *a priori* judgment.

As for the universe being self-subsisting, the problem is to produce the hydrogen. It seems scarcely credible, but this is done by "postulating" a hydrogen plant somewhere in the Milky Way which produces it out of nothing—and never goes on strike.

One important point arises from this. In order to deny the Christian conception of God the Creator, the intelligent atheist has to become a pantheist: it is the universe which has the divine attributes. He has freed himself from his Christian shackles only to fall back into paganism. And the new pantheism is no different from the old; the same tree bears the same fruit. One could find a thousand parallels to old Joe Stalin in pagan antiquity, but one could not parallel Francis of Assisi then or now. The Creator's natural law is no longer proclaimed, but we are as permissive of unnatural vice as were the ancient Greeks. Our new humanism practices infanticide on a scale unknown to Carthage. We fight shy of God revealed but are "in search" for the Unknown God. It is all the same, down to ridiculous details. The point scarcely needs labouring.

But surely the most extraordinary feature of the new pantheism is the revival of the Eternal Return. This was logical enough to the ancient pagans since they thought of the starry heavens as divine and governing the affairs of men. Since the heavens rotated, it only required their exact return to a previous position for everything on earth to be exactly the same. Jaki (page 29) gives a superb example from the Pythagorean, Eudemus. He warned his wretched pupils: "I shall converse with you, staff in hand, and you will sit as you are sitting now, and so it will be in everything else." Yes, but surely nobody believes that now? Come, come, that is precisely progressive thought! Have you no young friends who have become communists or Buddhists? That it is a dogma of Buddhism is known well enough. But, thanks to Engels and Blanqui, it is also a dogma of Marxism. It was also a basic idea of Nietzsche, that *enfant terrible* of the atheists, who proudly proclaimed himself "the European Buddhist." As he was the complete intellectual aristocrat (not to say snob), he would doubtless recant now that it has become fashionable. More extraordinary, those two pontiffs of the scientific world until so recently, Ernst Mach and Karl Popper, were both Eternal Return-ers—and the former even became a Buddhist.

One wonders what is the attraction of the Eternal Return:

"Round and round and round she goes. First her head and then her toes." It is not empirically provable. In theory it is not necessary to atheism although it fits in very neatly with pantheism. With all the caution of an historian of science, Professor Jaki suggests that the motive may be to exclude the once-for-all Incarnation and redemption of mankind. It could be so. But it is not science. It is pure prejudice.

The real trouble in cosmology for the atheist/pantheist, however, does not lie in his intellectual denials and postulates, but in how to popularize his ideals. Humans are not disembodied intellects. They believe in God for a great variety of inferential reasons. Notably, they find it difficult to imagine themselves as being purposeless. Then, from time to time they have feelings of awe, of wonderment, when confronted with the harmony and beauty of creation. Indeed, I knew an eminent surgeon who was a radical atheist. He was trying to restore a labourer's hand which had been badly squashed in an accident, when he was suddenly overwhelmed by the idea: "Here am I with all my intelligence, experience and techniques trying to botch up this unbelievably versatile instrument, the human hand, which I believe to have been made by accident." His conversion was only indirectly intellectual; it was primarily due to a feeling of awe. In fact, teleology—the argument from purpose and design—may be the least convincing of the Five Ways to God but it lends itself the most easily to a convincing argument *ad hominem*.

Herein lies the enormous importance of Darwin. I don't know when the word "evolution" was first used in connection with the cosmos—presumably in the eighteenth century. Anyway, it was common currency long before the 1859 publication of *The Origin of the Species*, in which work it does not happen to occur. Besides, the word is perfectly capable of an orthodox interpretation. The originality of Darwin is to have restricted the idea to "natural selection" and "the survival of the fittest." What he was doing was to substitute mechanical determinism for design and purpose. A means had been found to prevent people being struck with awe at the spectacle of creation: the universe was just complicated mechanics, an eternal industrial revolution based on *laissez-faire*.

I have referred to the originality of Darwin. In fact, he was not original at all: he was merely reviving the pre-Christian idea of the Stoics, in the same way as pantheism and the Eternal Return are revivals. In his *De Natura Deorum* Cicero was at pains to point out that no divine power is needed to explain order in the universe, *provided* one is willing to view it as spontaneous growth. This is exactly what Darwin did.

The virulent atheism of the eighteenth century *philosophes* had only affected the religious belief of the educated classes. It was too abstract for humble folk. But one could understand Darwin: it was all about birds and beetles. Popular irreligion dates from *The Origin of the Species*, 1859. It spread like wildfire. A little more than a generation later, in 1908, it seemed astonishing that so obviously normal an Englishmen as G.K. Chesterton should have the courage to publish his *Orthodoxy*.

It was in 1860, the year following the publication of *The Origin*, that Karl Marx wrote to Charles Darwin for permission to dedicate to him the English translation of *Das Kapital*. Darwin refused the honour—but Marx had understood the real import of *The Origin*. On December 13th, 1860, he wrote to Engels that it provided crucial support "for the class struggle in history." On the following January 16th he wrote to Lasalle that Darwin had dealt "a death blow to teleology in natural sciences." The fact is that Darwin and Marx—and Marx at least realised it—were preaching the same gospel: mechanical determinism. Marx was applying to history what Darwin was applying to biology. But it is the same system. They stand or fall together.

This explains why there is no fundamental opposition between the liberal West, dominated by Darwin, and the communist East, dominated by Marx. There can be plenty of practical, political dissent but no war of religion, because they have the same. The principal difference seems to be that in the East natural selection and the survival of the fittest are insured by genocide and the gulag, whereas in the West they are assured by abortion. There is certainly an altar to Moloch in the determinist Pantheon.

Incidentally the same applied to Hitler. We were all agreed about the survival of the fittest. We only disagreed as to who the fittest were or are. For the communist it is the Party; for Hitler it was the *Herrenvolk*; in the West we are to wait and see.

It exactly is exactly a century ago, in 1882, that Darwin died, as is known to every Englishman, since he has had to stick on an envelope Darwin's grizzly face, suitably surrounded by some equally extinct but clean-shaven reptiles. Since then, he has become the prophet of our brave, new world: taught in every school, preached in every university, proclaimed by the media. *The Descent of Man* is now one hundred and eleven years old and *The Origin of the Species* one hundred and twenty-three. Presumably, in that long time, a mass of incontrovertible evidence has accumulated to prove beyond any conceivable doubt that Darwin's daring hypotheses were true.

Actually, 1859 was rather an unfortunate date for the publication of *The Origin*. It was in the ensuing ten years that Pasteur laid the foundations of modern bacteriology—which was consequently unknown to Darwin. Worse still, in 1866 Mendel opened up the whole science of genetics by publishing his experiments on peas. The case of Mendel is particularly significant. It is perfectly clear that his findings imposed limits, to say the least, on natural selection. But by 1866 Darwin was already the supreme pontiff of the natural sciences. What was one to do with Mendel? Ignore him! This was done all the more easily as he happened to be a retrograde, Austrian, RC abbot. I have it on Doctor Bronowski's unimpeachable evidence that Mendel's experiments were never discussed at university level until some thirty-five years later, in the early 1900s. There was—and still is—a far harsher scientific Index than was ever the Index of the Holy Office. However, the point is that Darwin was ante-Mendelian if not antediluvian.

As was only to be expected, the implications arising from the work of Pasteur were examined first and foremost in France, if only because of the language difficulties. Mendel's peas consequently found the seed-ground well prepared. Hence the only steady opposition to Darwinian determinism, in biology in general and in botany and genetics in particular, has been and still is French. In this connection, Jaki (page 288) quotes the 1937 edition of the French Encyclopedia (volume five, pages 82–88): "It follows from what has been said that the theory of evolution is impossible... Evolution is a kind of dogma which its priests no longer believe in but continue to preach to the people. So much for a subject which one must have the courage to enunciate clearly, so that future generations should direct their research along different lines." Such a statement could not get into an encyclopedia in the U.S.A. and could not be expressed so bluntly in England. I shall return to the French scene in due course.

It was at much the same time as Mendel began to be taken seriously, at the start of the century, that doubt arose as to the eternity and infinity of the universe. In 1897, Max Planck's "quantum theory" not only supposed a finite quantity of energy, but "entropy" was precisely the measure of the energy which was not transferable. If all energy was not transferable, it became extremely difficult to see how the universe could be eternal.

Hot in the footsteps of Planck came Einstein. The curvature of light indicated that the universe was in fact finite; moreover it was expanding. Besides, light had an absolute speed, which made the time-space ratio a fourth dimension—as limiting and finite as the other three. Perhaps more important was his theory of general relativity. Although everything in the universe is entirely specific—as specific as our fingerprints—nonetheless everything is related in the time-space dimension. Just as "specificity" looks singularly like a scientific term for contingency, so does "general relativity" look suspiciously like teleology—order and purpose. It is consequently no longer surprising to find eminent scientists expressing a feeling of awe—a feeling incompatible with determinism.

In this connection, Jaki as usual has the apt quotation to hand (page 274). It is taken from Sir Bernard Lovell's presidential address to the British Association for the Advancement of Science on August 27th, 1975. Referring to the first second after the expansion of the universe had got underway, Sir Bernard said: "It is an astonishing reflection that if the interaction (of protons and neutrons) were only a few percent stronger, then all the hydrogen in the primeval condensate would have been turned into helium in the early stages of expansion. No galaxies, no stars, no life would have emerged. It would be a universe forever unknowable by living creatures." Yes, the reflection is astonishing. But more important, Sir Bernard admits to his astonishment. He has the natural reaction to teleology: awe.

Incidentally, it is not only in the Darwinian West that determinism has come under fire. In the Marxist East, cosmology as such has no longer been studied in the universities of the U.S.S.R. from 1936 onwards, precisely because it laid itself too open to metaphysics, that is to contingency and teleology. So much for the objectivity of Soviet science.

It is time I returned to France. Sooner rather than later everything in that wonderful country gets turned into politics. Opposition to atheistic determinism was clearly a clerical plot against the third Republic. Hence the extraordinary anti-Catholic laws of Waldeck-Rousseau and Combes at the start of the century. One of their results was to exile the French Jesuit novitiate to England. Suddenly these splendid, dedicated young men were exposed to the full blast of evolution, from which they had been protected in France. It is difficult for us to imagine the impact. We, the indigenous natives, accepted the irreligion of Darwin in the same vague sort of way that we accepted the religion of Anglicanism. As a little boy, it was in much the same spirit that I was hoiked off to visit the tomb of Saint Edward in Westminster Abbey and the Piltdown Skull in the Natural History Museum. We had been inoculated at an early age. Not so the young Jesuits.

It so happened that among these young Jesuits was a lyrical poet of the first order, one Teilhard de Chardin. Along with his poetic imagination he brought to evolution all the determination and heroism engendered by the *Spiritual Exercises*. The result is there for all to see: *The Phenomenon of Man*. His "mind-world" (or however else "noösphere" gets translated) without the Fall and sin, his point Omega without ever a point Alpha, is all pure determinism with a bit of poetic licence thrown in. The only evidence of theism in his cosmology is his point Omega: apparently he did not believe in the Eternal Return. The fact of the matter is that Teilhard was introducing mechanical determinism into religion just as Marx had introduced it into history, Darwin into biology and Spencer into physics. They are all foals from the same stable. Where he disagrees with the others is not in principle but in practice: to Teilhard the spearhead of the evolutionary process is not the Party, nor the *Herrenvolk*, nor the play of democracy, but religion.

This is not to deny Teilhard's personal piety. Indeed, he had the spirit of a medieval monk. He felt so certain of his facts that, if physical evidence was lacking, he was prepared to provide it. As the medieval monk produced false relics out of pure devotion and conviction, so has Teilhard given us the Piltdown Skull and Peking Man.

It would, of course, be absurd to imagine that Teilhard was the only priest to be caught up in the determinism of his age. His genius lay in expressing what is basically irreligion in religious terms. This is exactly what a great many people want: the worst of both worlds. His success was therefore astonishing, and all round us we witness the result. It is not unusual to meet Marxist Jesuits, evolutionary Benedictines, free-thinking bishops. But the trouble really lies deeper than such manifestations.

We have disconnected the notions of "religion" and "truth," which Christianity had united. We have become a "pilgrim Church" and wander round in search for truth and the shrine of the Unknown God. Having lost the notion of God the Creator, and consequently of a natural law other than our conscience, we have become tolerant of every error. And, since man is no longer made in the image of God, we have grown intolerant of persons. We have ceased to think of the creation as God-made and good, to be treated with awe and respect, but as a fortuitous event on which we mechanically improve. The Latin word *salus* has returned to its pagan meaning of "health" and "well-being" in this world, not the Christian meaning of salvation in the next. We even proclaim that we expect a Return, the Second Coming; but it is because we recoil from the first, the once-for-all Incarnation and Redemption. And so on. It is fundamental religious attitudes which have changed, so fundamental that few people seem to have noticed them.

What seems odd, however, is that so many ecclesiastics should have found the entrance to mechanical determinism at the very moment that the scientists, the natural philosophers, have discovered the exit. However, as I said at the start of this lecture, irreligion is a by-product of Christianity. It is not, therefore, surprising to find it in the Christian Church. Indeed, those who know what religion is about are the best qualified to deny it.

Unwanted Priest

I closed my lecture at the Centre Charlier with a display of some anti-religious posters. They came from two distinct sources.

I had picked up the first group in 1931 from an upper school in Moscow. They are forcefully designed but the content is rather naive. They are anti-clerical rather than anti-religious. A typical example is one for use in a history class, already mentioned in chapter one, but worth mentioning again. It represents the square in front of Notre-Dame de Paris with the cathedral in the background. To the right is a leering capitalist, identifiable by his top hat, in front of whom are Cardinal Verdier (Archbishop of Paris in 1931) and Marshal Foch, who are encouraging some troops on the left side of the poster to massacre a crowd of defenceless workers. Underneath is a quotation from Karl Marx referring to the Paris Commune of 1870/71.

Now it is obvious that the religion might still be true even if cardinals were in the habit of mowing down the populace. As anti-religious propaganda it is naive. What is wicked and typically communist about the poster is its falsification of history. It so happens that in May 1871 it was the then Archbishop of Paris, Georges Darboy, who while in prison was murdered in cold blood by the communists. As I said before, you do not just tell a lie but the exact opposite of the truth; it leaves your opponent speechless. It is the technique used so successfully by progressives when they accuse traditionalists of being divisive.

The second group of posters I had acquired in 1981/82 from church porches in France. Although it seems invidious to make a choice, perhaps the most remarkable of these was issued by FOCS, the official organ of the French hierarchy for religious propaganda. It was to be seen in most French churches during the second half of 1981. I removed my copy from the cathedral at Viviers.

The poster is attractively designed by one Patrick O'Heguerty, presumably a devout Irish artist. In the middle it portrays the cruciform figure of a man in outline, arms outstretched and feet together. But there is no cross behind the figure, and the outline indicates that the man is wearing jacket and trousers. It is not

158

Jesus Christ at all but a gentleman (the local P.P.?) skipping for joy in a meadow strewn with flowers. Over his head is written *la santé*—health. In large capitals at the bottom of the poster is the text: *L'homme vivant c'est la gloire de Dieu*—"living man, that is God's glory." I need scarcely point out the blasphemy: Health instead of Salvation; a dancing clown instead of the sacrifice of the Cross; living man as the glory of God instead of the death of Jesus as the salvation of mankind. (Incidentally, the text is a truncated quotation from Saint Irenaeus; the full text reads: "Living man, that is God's glory—but the life of man is the vision of God.") Only a priest could have thought of it. Only the authority of the legitimate hierarchy could have ensured its display in every church. No communist, poor fool, could have conceived such dire irreligion.

Yes, irreligion is an inevitable by-product of the true religion. It seems, however, a pity that the Church should display the by-product and hide the truth.

17

The Suffering Laity

By 1983, twenty years had passed since the Spirit of the Council had started to blow. It had blown away everything which could be recognised as Catholic, from the pope's tiara to Friday fish. Moreover, there seemed no respite to the storm. I should have to resign myself to being an unwanted, unemployed priest for the rest of my life. But, by divine Providence, a priest I was. I could consequently say the old Mass, recite the old breviary and generally satisfy my religious convictions. The people for whom I felt immensely sorry were the wretched laity. They were at the mercy of progressive priests and expected to cheer at every change. The worst sufferers were obviously parents, who could no longer guarantee transmitting their religion to their children. The callous cruelty of bishops and priests appalled me. I knew of none who had shown any practical commiseration. I consequently decided to write a book myself which would illustrate a little of the sadness and misery caused by what had happened in the Church. It is a novel called *Judith's Marriage*. Here is its dedicatory forward.

I was ordained a priest on March 31st, 1940. In June of that year, I was appointed to Slough, an industrial suburb of London, where I founded Saint Anthony's parish in the dormitory to the Trading Estate. In September 1954 I was moved to the parish of Saint Edmund at Bury St Edmunds, the county town of West Suffolk, where I remained until Saturday, November 29th, 1969. I resigned and retired as from midnight on that day. Why? Because on the following morning, the first Sunday of Advent, the new *ordo* of Mass was supposed to come into force.

"But surely," one may say, "you were being rather intransigent over a bit of mumbo-jumbo?" Perhaps. But it happened to be the touchstone to a basic issue. This issue was that the new reforms in general and of the liturgy in particular were based on the assumption that the Catholic laity were a set of ignorant fools. They practised out of tribal custom; their veneration of the Cross and the Mass was totem-worship; they were motivated by nothing more than the fear of hell; their piety was superstition and their loyalty, habit. But the most gratuitous insult of all was that most Catholics had a Sunday religion which in no way affected their weekly behaviour. This monstrous falsehood was—and still is—maintained by bishops and priests who, for the most part, have never been adult laymen. Every day the Catholic workman had to put up with the jeers of his colleagues, as the more educated with their sneers. Every night they took their religion to bed with them.

I am not in a position to judge other priests' parishioners. I am, however, in a position to judge what were my own. No words are adequate for me to express my admiration for the conscious faith and piety of my flock, both in Slough and in Bury. This is where the trouble lay. The reforms were based on criticism; I was unwilling to take any action which might make me appear to criticise the wonderful people whom I was ordained to serve. I was perfectly conscious that I learned more about God from them than they were likely to learn from me.

Then there were the converts. I happened to be one myself. The mystery of grace is consequently not absent from my mind. I have no notion of the number I received. A couple of hundred? Perhaps more. They ranged from the highly cultured to, quite literally, tramps. To all I gave the same eternal truths. Perhaps it is pride, but I am unwilling to admit that I deceived them into the Church.

And the marriage converts. This is a breed which is normally despised. I have it in writing in the hand of a bishop. How I admired them! Of course, human love has some analogy with divine Love, or God would not have rooted it so firmly in the human make-up. I suppose I could class myself as an "intellectual convert." What does that mean? Merely that the bankruptcy of my intelligence was filled by God's grace. Marriage converts have more than I to show: their human love looks towards divine Love. And they are willing to prove it by an acid test: the creative act. How can anyone despise such people?

Perhaps the reason for my resignation is now clear: I was unwilling to be instrumental in any change which might cause scandal to my wonderful parishioners.

What passes belief is that I know of no book or article published within the last twenty years extolling the virtues and commiserating the sufferings of the Catholic laity. If they dared to remonstrate, they were merely told that they were divisive, disloyal and disobedient. Hence the present novel. Its purpose is to show that at any rate one priest appreciates the predicament into which the laity have been put.

I consequently dedicate this little work to my erstwhile parishioners at Slough and at Bury St Edmunds. It is a small token of my admiration for their loyalty to the faith and of my gratitude for the example of unquestioning piety which they set me.

Perhaps my forward sounds a bit pathetic—but it is perfectly true.

Anyway, *Judith's Marriage* is the story of an heroic marriage convert—but it is far more than that. It contains a good deal of fundamental theology, both dogmatic and moral. Moreover, I think I have managed to portray how religion works in people. Because it does work: it influences what we love and hate—and consequently most of our actions. Of course, we and our non-Catholic brethren may look as like as two peas, but the Catholic does have different attitudes. At the very least he will have divine Providence at the back of his mind: that "other world" which somehow controls this.

I myself think *Judith's Marriage* a very good book—far more profound than *Mitre and Crook*—although, in the French edition, *Mitre and Crook* sold over twice the number of *Judith*. Concerning the English edition of *Judith*, a friend of mine got hold of "the most brilliant young publisher in America" who, after four years delay, in 1987, having printed a thousand copies, went bankrupt and disappeared. It is a beautifully produced volume and will one day become a collector's rarity.[1]

1 *Judith's Marriage* was republished by Angelico Press in 2020.

18

Monsignor Lefebvre

I think it is time that I dealt with Monsignor Lefebvre. As I have said, I have met him quite often—in London, at Flavigny, at Écône and Richeranche. However, I only know him rather superficially.

He certainly looks like the ideal bishop: a good and kindly man. His appearance is all in his favour. He has a streak of humility, strange in a man so stubborn. In the early 1970s, his representative in England, one Father Morgan, put up for the committee of the Latin Mass Society. I wrote immediately to Lefebvre pointing out that this was clean contrary to the agreement at the Kenworthy-Browns'. Lefebvre answered me by return of post saying that he had asked Morgan to desist. Why should he pay the slightest attention to me? This is an example of pure humility.

On the other hand, I think he is very gullible. For instance, during the course of his retreat at Flavigny he mentioned that before the Council there were 250,000 converts per year to Catholicism in England. Doubtless someone had told him that there were about 250,000 converts altogether and he mistook it to be converts per year. I went along to his room to correct him. The maximum number received per year was just over 15,000—already a very large number. But if a quarter of a million were received per year there would soon be a staggering lack of Anglicans and nonconformists. No, no! That is what he had heard and he was sure it was true. I doubt if I managed to convince him, but at least he promised not to use the statistic again.

I also think that he is not a very good judge of character. I have noticed several excellent young men and a few professors who have left him. He seems entirely surrounded by "yes men."

In fact, I think Monsignor Lefebvre a very good man but rather a stupid one.

On August 27th, 1987 I wrote an article on Lefebvre's proposed consecration of bishops. I sent it to an English and a French review but neither published it; both thought it would only add fuel to the fire. However, I publish it here to illustrate my attitude a full year before Lefebvre actually consecrated.

New Code of Canon Law, Canon 1382: "Both the bishop who, without a pontifical mandate, consecrates a person a bishop, and the one who receives consecration from him, incur a *latae sententiae* excommunication reserved to the Apostolic See."

I do not propose to judge the character of a man as holy, guileless, frank and French as Archbishop Lefebvre. My object is restricted to the present problem of his consecration of one or more bishops.

It is perfectly clear that over the past twenty years Lefebvre's primary preoccupation has changed along with time and events. His first preoccupation was the preservation of the immemorial Mass. This inevitably evolved into ordaining priests to say it. At first came his house of studies at Fribourg, which was closed down through no fault of Lefebvre, as far as I know. So Écône was founded as a self-contained seminary with its staff, theologians and experts. Quite apart from Monsignor Lefebvre's unfortunate suspension in 1975, which would only increase the "self-containedness," the very fact of Écône altered the nature of Lefebvre's opposition. The emphasis shifted from *defence* of the immemorial Mass to *attack* on neo-modernism in general and Vatican II in particular. This has finally crystallised into "religious liberty," a thorny problem of social philosophy which has little to do with divine revelation. To understand the "Lefebvre problem" this evolution must be borne in mind. He started as the lone bishop to defend what is most sublime in the Christian religion— the Mass; he has become the only bishop, in a self-contained ecclesial group, to fight religious liberty.

Quite apart from this metamorphosis, Lefebvre himself has

grown older. The question of his episcopal successor has been on people's minds for some ten years. The preoccupation became acute after the failure of negotiations between Ratzinger and Lefebvre in 1982.

However, it was only on May 13th, 1986 that I heard of Lefebvre's positive intention to consecrate. The consecration was to take place on October 26th, the feast of Christ the King, during the Assisi prayer-party. The information was given to me on exceptionally reliable authority. My informant had heard it at least a month previously but this was the first time he had an opportunity to visit me, and he did not wish to commit the matter to paper. Curiously enough, the news was confirmed twice during the following month from entirely different sources, one from Paris and the other from Switzerland.

The rumour acquired considerable force when it was learned that the principal subject of Lefebvre's retreat to his priests at Écône in September 1986 was "the possibility and liceity of episcopal consecrations and the status and functions of such bishops." There was nothing secret about this retreat, but, unfortunately, I have not got a copy of it. I am certain of its existence since Father Aulagnier, the superior of the French Lefebvrists, refers to it in the introductory letter to his bulletin of January 1987. It would, of course, be natural for Lefebvre to give some guidelines to his priests concerning the role of the bishops whom he intended to consecrate on October 26th.

But there was no such consecration on October 26th. I felt so sure of my information that at first I presumed him to have consecrated secretly. But I discarded such an idea. Lefebvre may have his faults, but he is incapable of such deceit.

Just over a month later came the bombshell. On December 2nd, 1986, Archbishop Lefebvre and Bishop De Castro-Mayer issued their joint declaration from Buenos Aires. The consecration of bishops is not referred to directly, but it is implied in the first sentence: "Rome has inquired whether we intended to announce our severance from the Vatican in view of the Assisi congress." This inquiry must have preceded the prayer-party, and the "severance from the Vatican" refers to his excommunication upon Lefebvre's consecration of a bishop on October 26th.

The next sentence gives Lefebvre's answer: "We feel that the sentence should rather be formulated as follows: 'Do you believe and intend to proclaim that by the Assisi congress the Roman authorities have completely severed themselves from the Catholic Church?'" Allowance must of course be made for hysterical polemics, but even so... The document continues in the same tone to the bitter end. However, the astonishing effusion of paragraph ten is worth recording: "This severance from the previous magisterium of the Church reached its climax at Assisi—after the visit to the synagogue. One shudders with horror at this public sin against the oneness of God, against the Incarnate Word and his Church." We shall see presently the probable prototype of this purple passage. In the meantime, it is worth meditating on the slightly different reactions such a statement is likely to produce on the simple faithful, on the reasonably educated and on its intended targets—John Paul II and Cardinal Ratzinger.

We now come to a document which I cannot date. My copy bears January 1987—but that is the date of its publication in the bulletin of the Confraternity of Saint Pius X. Internal evidence indicates that it existed before the retreat of September 1986.

It is a very long article of nearly thirty pages of ordinary print. It was issued by Father Aulagnier. Clearly the theologians of Écône—whom, for brevity, I shall in future call the Écônemists—have been hard at work. The article is an analysis of the relevant chapter (XXI) on episcopal consecrations in Dom Gréa's work on *The Church and Her Divine Constitution*.

Dom Gréa was indeed a distinguished theologian at the end of the last century. His work has even been republished as recently as 1965. He was perfectly orthodox, although not a rigid "papalist." Thus, he admitted that his views were not shared by such staunch Jesuits as Bellarmine and Suárez. I shall not bother the reader with details in the Écônemists' article—such as the misquotations by omission and a highly dubious translation. The crux of the matter is sufficiently clear to any layman.

All are agreed that there are two distinct but essential elements in episcopal consecration: firstly, the sacrament, which is always valid, even if conferred illicitly; secondly, the Apostolic mission (i.e., jurisdiction), which can only be given by the pope as pastor of the whole Flock. Agreed? Yes! Dom Gréa, in the way theologians will, asks the question: Is there any hypothetical case in which a bishop, as successor of the Apostles, could in fact transfer jurisdiction on his own authority without recourse to Rome? Gréa's answer is yes—provided three conditions are fulfilled: 1. that our holy religion is in danger of extinction; 2. that in fact there are no longer any bishops to fulfil the "Apostolic mission"; 3. that recourse to the Holy See is in fact impossible.

One does not have to be endowed with abnormal penetration to see that the Éconemists can interpret these conditions very differently from Dom Gréa's intention. Gréa was thinking of the Arian persecutions in Asia Minor, when the Catholics had been practically wiped out, when all bishops had been killed or fled, when recourse to the Holy See was physically impossible. To the Éconemist the present situation is identical: Catholicism has been wiped out by Vatican II and the Assisi prayer-party; apart from Monsignor Lefebvre there is not a bishop who fulfils the Apostolic mission; recourse to the Holy See is impossible since it will no longer listen to the magisterium of Écône.

Unfortunately, this theological dispute has been settled once and for all. Gréa's hypothetical conditions have been fulfilled within my lifetime. This occurred in communist China in the mid-1950s. The surviving bishops consecrated and appointed bishops to the vacant sees on their own authority since the government would not allow them to communicate with Rome. On June 29th, 1958, in his encyclical *Ad Apostolorum Principis*, Pius XII excommunicated consecrators and consecrated alike. This implies that under no circumstances, even if Don Gréa's conditions are fulfilled, can episcopal consecrations be made without permission of the Holy See. The encyclical ends on a rather formidable tone: "These consecrations are so grievous an outrage against the very unity of the Church as to entail automatic excommunication reserved specifically to the Holy See..." It reads like the prototype of Lefebvre's excommunication of the Church in December 1986.

The next move is Lefebvre's *Letter to His Priests*. It is dated April 27th, 1987, but was not published until June/July. It is a sober document. The tactics have completely changed: Gréa does not get so much as a mention. The new approach is expressed with commendable clarity in paragraph eleven: "Since we lack canonical 'mission,' we have no jurisdiction in fact on that score, but in law the Church grants us jurisdiction in view of the duty of the faithful to sanctify themselves through the grace of the sacraments which (otherwise than through us) they would receive with difficulty or doubtfully... We thus receive jurisdiction in each particular case to come to the help of souls in need."

What a difference can be made by tone and style! The above argument seems cogent merely because it is so well expressed. But in actual fact it does not work. It is not the "souls in need" who grant faculties or jurisdiction to a priest who lacks them; it is the Church which grants them to priests "in good standing" who happen to lack them, in view of "souls in need." This does not apply to excommunicated priests and to suspended priests. Otherwise, excommunication and suspension would have no meaning at all.

I do not wish to labour the point, but a few corollaries should be pointed out. Jurisdiction from pastoral care (i.e., the needs of the faithful) is highly "progressive." It no longer springs from our Holy Mother the Church but from the People of God. Any validly ordained priest would only have to find a couple of "souls in need" to give him jurisdiction. It would not merely be Lefebvre's bishops and priests who acquired jurisdiction, but the odd fifty bishops and umpteen priests ordained directly or indirectly by the late Archbishop of Hue.[1] Then there would be the Jansenists, the Old Catholics, a host of Orientals, Anglicans, Lutherans and other Protestants who happen to have valid orders. It seems strange to find Lefebvre on the side of the ecumenists. But it does not work. The juridical Church is either visible or invisible. It is the Church of Rome or it does not exist at all.

So far Lefebvre's letter has only dealt with the justification of his clergy's ministry through "souls in need." Had he nothing to say about episcopal consecrations? Yes, he had. Out of twenty-nine paragraphs it is mentioned once, and forms the tiny paragraph twenty-three. Here it is: "But if it were necessary one day

1 Archbishop Ngô Đình Thục.

to consecrate bishops, their only episcopal function would be to confer holy orders; they would have no power of jurisdiction since they would lack canonical 'mission.'" That is all. It is difficult to know what Lefebvre means by this sibylline a statement. Gone is justification by pastoral care: a candidate for the episcopacy is scarcely a "soul in need," no matter how much he may desire a mitre. Does Monsignor Lefebvre really imagine that he can avoid excommunication by separating the sacrament of consecration from ecclesiastical jurisdiction? The fact of consecrating is a juridical act on the part of the consecrator; and the person consecrated recognises his jurisdiction. More could be said on that score, but that is quite enough.

The *Letter*, although dated April 27th, was circulated to coincide with Monsignor Lefebvre's ordination ceremony at Écône on June 29th, 1987. However, neither it nor Dom Gréa get a mention in his famous sermon on that occasion. But there is a new note in the sermon: Lefebvre's charismatism. "I have occasionally mentioned that in order to perform what I judge necessary to preserve the continuity of the Catholic Church I was waiting for a sign from divine Providence. I must admit to being satisfied that such signs have been vouchsafed. What are they? There are two: Assisi and the reply from Rome to our objections on the score of religious liberty." As providential signs they appear quite fantastic. It would be preferable to place more trust in divine Providence and less in signs of one's own choice.

Like most sermons, Lefebvre's is fairly repetitive. Three times he repeats his intention to consecrate bishops:

"That is why I shall probably appoint successors to continue this work, since Rome is shrouded in darkness. At the present time Rome can no longer hear the voice of truth..."

"That is why, if God asks it of us, we shall not hesitate to appoint auxiliaries to continue this work..."

"That is why it is probable that I shall consecrate bishops before I must render to God an account of my life."

The phrase "that is why" which opens each statement does not refer to any theological or canonical justification but to Lefebvre's belief that Rome is shrouded in darkness and is incapable of hearing the voice of truth. We are back to Lefebvre's attitude as contained in the Buenos Aires declaration of December 1986: he needs no justification since Rome has already excommunicated herself.

Moreover, this attitude was not a fantasy emitted in the heat of a sermon. It was repeated, specified and underlined a fortnight later on July 12th. According to *Le Monde* of July 14th, Lefebvre stopped off at Rimini on his way to Rome for his interview with Cardinal Ratzinger. At Rimini Lefebvre is reported to have made two significant statements: 1. he intended to give Rome "six months or a year" to reach agreement over his consideration of a bishop; 2. he was not worried about his excommunication since "to be excommunicated by the Catholic Church which is no longer truly Catholic is in no way sinful."

Presuming the accuracy of *Le Monde*'s report, these two pronouncements are highly significant. In the first place, Lefebvre reserves to himself the right to threaten Rome with schism whenever he likes—and could not care less. Is there not a word for "pressure by threat"? Secondly, Lefebvre is not worried about excommunication because he has already excommunicated the Vatican with all its works, pomps and temptations. To him, Rome is the Scarlet Woman of the Apocalypse just as it was to Luther.

Two days later, on July 14th, there was the interview with Ratzinger. All we know about it is that it was "frank and sincere." This is diplomatic language for "bellicose and without agreement." We can consequently fear the worst.

This is as far as my documentation went when I started to write this article on August 27th. Incomplete as it may be, it does raise some important questions.

So long as Lefebvre was defending the concrete issue of the immemorial Mass, a settlement with the Vatican always seemed possible. But once he turned to the attack—and this on progressively widened abstract problems such as neo-modernism, Vatican II and religious liberty—the chances of a settlement became progressively remote.

The attack on religious liberty is particularly complex and abstract. It might help if it were put into concrete terms. The fact of the matter is in the West we have "anti-religious liberty"; in the East we have "anti-religious constraint." This situation is as disastrous as it is unprecedented. The alternatives are clear: "religious liberty" as expounded by John Paul II or "religious constraint" as formulated by Lefebvre. The trouble with the latter is how it could possibly be implemented and whether in practice it would not supply ammunition to "anti-religious liberty and constraint." Such is the concrete problem. But I fail to see how Lefebvre and the Vatican can possibly come to agreement in the abstract. It is very sad.

In the meantime, Lefebvre can threaten to consecrate every six months. The initiative is in his hands. This situation must change. It is rumoured that a Roman document is in preparation. Its production should be accelerated. All that is "concrete" in Lefebvre's opposition—the immemorial Mass and his devoted priests—should be safeguarded to the absolute limit of possibility. All that is theoretic and abstract, including religious liberty and constraint, should be left to sort itself out.

There was another problem. In his Buenos Aires declaration of December 1986, in his sermon at Écône on June 29th and in his interview at Rimini on July 12th, 1987, Lefebvre excommunicates the Church of Rome. But is it the Church one excommunicates or oneself? The Church is not an object for discussion but an object of faith: "I believe in the Holy Ghost, the Holy Catholic Church..."; "and in One, Holy, Catholic and Apostolic Church."

Since I started this article with a canon, I might as well close it with another.

New Code, Canon 1373: "A person who publicly incites his or her subjects to hatred or animosity against the Apostolic See or the Ordinary because of some act of ecclesiastical authority or ministry, or who provokes the subjects to disobedience against them, is to be punished by interdict or other just penalties."

Lefebvre consecrated his bishops on June 30th, 1988. I have three remarks to make on that score.

Primarily and most important, it exhibits in Monsignor Lefebvre a complete distrust of God's divine Providence. Indeed, all along he has shown slightly too much trust in himself. This has now reached the climax of excommunication.

Secondly, Lefebvre represented the tradition of the Church. That was the basis of his popularity. By consecrating bishops against the authority of the Holy See he has acted contrary to a fundamental tradition of the juridical Church. He has become an anti-traditionalist.

Thirdly, can Lefebvre not see that if Rome recognised his bishops, any progressive bishop or episcopal conference could consecrate bishops at will? And that would be the end of the RC Church! If he cannot see that, then he is totally senile—and should consult an oculist.

Then there are two very disconcerting quotations given by Monsieur Jean Madiran in Number 336 of his review *Itinéraires*.

In the June number of *Le Choc*, Lefebvre is reported to have said: "Jean Madiran, who was incapable this time of making the right choice, says that he wants to stay in the visible Church. *But we are the visible Church!*"

In the circular of Credo Association Monsignor Lefebvre repeats himself more explicitly: "Jean Madiran criticises us and says that we don't belong to the visible Church. On the contrary, it is we who are the Church, a branch of the Church—powerful; and today we display the visibility of the Church: its unity, catholicity, apostolicity, holiness… Where do you find those marks among the others? It is we who bear the marks of the visible Church; it is the others who no longer belong to it."

So, Lefebvre no longer claims to belong to the Church because he claims to be the Church. I fear that the old gentleman must have gone mad.

The old gentleman may have gone senile, but this certainly does not apply to his young followers. They attack as traitors anybody who accepted Rome's offer—as made to Monsignor Lefebvre—of the old Mass and sacramental forms. The diatribes and false statements made against Dom Gérard Calvet and Monsieur Jean Madiran here in France are quite appalling. Of course, we all know that the French love polemics and even invective. But we also know that those who use them are usually in the wrong.

Enough about Lefebvre.

19

Some Correspondence

It may well be imagined that as a "resistance priest," but unaffili-
ated with Monsignor Lefebvre, I received a vast amount of correspondence. I answered all letters from people whom I knew but
very few from those I did not. The first two letters date from
April and May 1986. They express only a tiny portion of the compassion I feel for the laity on whom the change of religion has
been imposed.

To a disconsolate Lady. April 11th, 1986.

My dear Lady,

I come to your letter of March 11th. You are over seventy and I
seventy-five. We both suffer from heart trouble. This is not surprising. It is symptomatic: we both suffer from broken hearts.
Both of us are converts, and with the totality of our hearts we
loved the Church to which we had surrendered. Until a couple of
years ago we still had some optimism and our hearts still ticked.
We could legitimately imagine that we might live long enough to
see some order re-established in the Church we love. No longer
now. We shall die in exile "beside the waters of Babylon": you
despised, myself rejected.

For sixteen years you have been battling heroically for the
immemorial Mass. For sixteen years I have been an unwanted
priest. But in both cases it has been a rather long and tedious "Stations of the Cross"—crucified between the Church we love and
the Mass in which we adore. And, in our ages and conditions, it

will end in death. How wonderful! Humanly speaking, Jesus was not a success since He died crucified. So shall we. In fact, the Christian religion is basically the divine triumph of human failure.

I was deeply moved by your letter. Since it was written long-hand I presume that you have not kept a copy, so I quote you verbatim: "What I find so distressing is the loss of daily Mass at any time between seven to eight or earlier; and to have the church open with a tabernacle in front of which to adore. If only it would come back I could say *nunc dimittis* and turn my face to the wall... Also, the turbulence in the Church has checked the spiritual growth one should or could have acquired in old age... I am always organising Mass somewhere—finding a priest, hunting for equipment, arranging transport. There is no peace. Also, no regularity—which the spiritual masters and classics lay down as vital. Will we *ever* have a chance to prepare ourselves for God as we had imagined we would have been able to do?"

No, my dear, you will not be able to prepare for death as you imagined you would. You will prepare for it by organising Mass, finding a priest, hunting for equipment and arranging transport.

Of course, being a priest I do not suffer directly as you do. I celebrate the divine Mysteries as and when I like. Even if nobody else is present, Jesus is always there. I have him to myself. It is wonderful! I do not suffer. My sorrow is desperately deep, but it is compassion for the laity, for you, deprived of the liturgy you love and unable to supply it yourselves. It is tragic. It is cruel.

However, I do carry a little burden of almost direct suffering. It is to be the helpless witness of the auto-destruction of the Church by my fellow priests. The vast majority of them are such decent, good men. I have never been and am not anticlerical. I love my "brethren of the cloth." Yet they are destroying all the expressions of my faith with a song in their heart.

Of course, there was an easy way out. Since my brethren, from pope to curate, were discarding the expressions of my faith, I was at liberty to discard its substance. My conversion, my priesthood, my cure of souls were just a few more of my numerous mistakes in life—albeit rather basic ones. It was in the spring of 1970. Since nobody wanted me to express my faith, I might as well chuck it overboard. In a desultory sort of way I tried to lose it. But faith is not merely a subjective assent; it is also an objective gift—which sticks like a limpet. Try as I might, I could not shake it off. I still believe in the divine Institution of Holy Church with the same enthusiasm as on the day of my reception, over fifty-two years ago. I still celebrate the divine Mysteries with the same adoration as I did forty-six years back at my first Mass.

I write about myself, but it is intended for you. We are both converts who have kept intact the faith of our conversion. We may be fools, my dear, but we have not been dishonourable; we have not rejected the grace which God has given.

I sum up. We are old and heartbroken. We are unlikely to live long enough to see order re-established in Holy Church. The human optimism which legitimately inspired us until a couple of years ago has been shattered. What is left to us is the theological virtue of blind hope.

All the expressions of our faith have been destroyed and derided by your priests and my brethren. What is left to us is the theological virtue of bare faith.

But we believe in the triumph of failure!

Devotedly…

The following letter, with a few personal touches and appropriate alterations, I sent to several childless correspondents—young priests or aged spinsters.

Neither you nor I are the chief sufferers in the present turmoil for the simple reason that we have no children. Humans are singularly resilient animals and can put up with a great deal of punishment. But to suffer in one's children and one's children's children is a very different matter. And this suffering falls on traditionalists and conformists alike. I wonder how many Catholic couples of the Roman rite there are in all the world who can be reasonably certain that their offspring will have the same religion as themselves, in outlook and in practice?

177

Actually, traditionalists stand a better chance to preserve their "outlook" than the rest. Tradition is not nostalgia for the past, but precisely the transmission of one's inheritance in the future. My feet are on a carpet, my bottom on a chair and this piece of paper on a desk, all of which I have inherited. I have no nostalgia about them and am grateful to have received them. But I very much hope to leave them in reasonable condition to my heirs. In fact, I am more concerned about their future than their past. Traditionalists in religion have at least preserved an outlook which they can transmit. Our progressive brethren, however, have squandered their inheritance in riotous living with ecumenicity, inculturation, charismatism and impure worldliness. They have nothing to transmit apart from their pathological hatred for gratitude, for acknowledging that they have received anything, be it from tradition, the Church or God. They are creators and redeemers, not receivers and redeemed.

As for "religious practice," humanly speaking I cannot conceive it lasting long in either camp. Among traditionalists there will be a lack of priests—and of any unifying principle. Among the conformists, the shortage of priests will be aggravated by the fact that "the tradition of practice" will disappear along with all other traditions.

Such is the problem which parents have to face, but from which a celibate clergy is immune. Therein lies the real tragedy.

No, my dear Father, we must not moan. We are really very lucky. We only have to face death. Parents face an abyss for their children.

I wonder, however, when the pope, cardinals, synods, bishops, abbots, monsignori, religious superiors, deans, canons and reverend fathers will realize how much gratuitous suffering they have inflicted? Probably never. They will face the Judgment with a smug smile of self-satisfaction. They will have succeeded! In what? In destroying the Mass and possibly the Church.

I publish these two letters because they illustrate a point which I fail to understand. In the Christian religion it is taken for granted that one should show a modicum of charity, avoid causing pain, alleviate suffering and so on. But here is the Catholic Church being totally uncharitable, causing acute pain to its devotees and avoiding by every means available to it alleviating the suffering which it itself has caused. And this not for six months or a year but for twenty-five years! It is preposterous. It is strange enough to find a couple of thousand bishops and several hundreds of thousands of priests conniving at this propagation of suffering, but what is really remarkable is that the sufferers still recognise the Church, still believe in Her, still love Her. This is really miraculous. One would have expected them to have given up their faith or to have joined Monsignor Lefebvre in his cosy little traditionalist group. Not a bit of it! The vast majority remain loyal to Holy Mother Church, no matter how scurvily she may treat us.

I myself furnish an excellent example of how curious is this situation. For over twenty years I have been retired in the diocese of Viviers. The diocese contains the eastern slopes of the Massif Central as the mountains come down to the Rhône valley. This implies numerous villages—and consequently parishes—cut off from their neighbours by sharp valleys or high ridges. But in twenty years over a third of the clergy have died and there is practically no one to replace them. The local bishop, moreover, is a perfectly agreeable man. But it does not cross his mind to ask me to supply in a priestless village. Why? Because I should say the old Mass and *no Mass* is better than that! It is the Mass, not I, which is rejected.

The next letter is much less important. It merely has to deal with a theological question of a young priest. Mind you, I have had to use it several times with a few changes, because progressives always raise the same objections, since they all read the same reviews. Anyway, it is a good example of how I have to spend my time. I translate from the French.

July 5th, 1987.

Dear Father,

I normally do not answer letters from unknown people concerning my publications. If I did, I should not have time to say Mass or brush my teeth. But you introduce yourself as recommended by Claude Martingay. I consequently owe you deference at least. But I warn you that I shall write as the ideas come to me.

I start off with your criticisms.

1. "I fail to understand your total opposition to the new Eucharistic prayers." The reason is very simple: there is no longer a "Roman liturgy." The three anaphoras (canons) of which you speak were immediately followed by two others for "children" and for "reconciliation"—plus endless permissions. The new Order of Mass has never existed: there are as many "new Orders" as there are celebrants. You write: "I am against all the new prayers which have since appeared." By what right? They have as much authority and more experience than the first ones.

2. "Nothing prevents the Church from promulgating new Eucharistic prayers." This is perfectly true theologically and juridically—but it is absolutely false *morally*. Who has given the Church permission to ride roughshod over the feelings of hundreds of millions of Catholics? It is an unmitigated sin of pride, of arrogance. The pope can invent a new Mass-form every morning before breakfast, but he has no right to impose it on the faithful, who are the heirs of Christ's testament.

3. "The Canon emerged out of several Eucharistic prayers." Of course it did. But why did nobody get upset? Because neither its "spirit" nor its visible and sensible form had changed until the Protestant Reformation and the Reformation of 1969. It was in 1969 that the "spirit" and the "form" of Mass changed—and there was a revolution: instead of being a sacrifice at which the Blessed Sacrament was made, it became the Eucharist, the making of the Blessed Sacrament without any sacrifice.

4. "The ancient tradition of Hippolytus" is not a tradition at all; it is archaeology. As far as my memory serves me, the writings of this heretical antipope were only rediscovered in about 1850. It is the same with your "Offertory... taken from the ritual

of the synagogue." Doubtless such texts are not bad in themselves. What is bad about them is that they have been used to destroy the Mass of the Roman Church.

5. Indirectly you admit the real problem at the bottom of your first page when you write: "Although I prefer the Roman Canon..." All honour to you—but you do not appear to have drawn any conclusion from your preference. *The Mass* was an inexorable fact—as are all things created by God's Providence (my solitary nose or my two ears). Now, it has become the subject of human choice. It is no longer divine since it depends on human preference. Is Mass *the* Mass or is it *a* Mass, the choice of the celebrant?

6. This brings me to a problem which has received too little attention. Canon 1247 insists that the faithful should attend Sunday Mass. But the celebrant can celebrate the Eucharist according to his own "preferences"—since you yourself do it. Can the layman refrain from attending Mass because the celebrant chooses a Eucharist other than the one he prefers? This is in fact what happens—and the churches empty. You, the celebrant, have no right to impose your preference on the faithful—who cannot celebrate themselves. In any case, you are imposing your wretched self precisely in the divine Act when you should disappear.

7. You say you are against the translations. I am all in favour of them. They illustrate the average intelligence of our national hierarchies. The worst is the French. French "good taste" is proverbial but French "bad taste" is peerless. The English runs it pretty close. The Italian is better and the German almost good. These are the only languages on which I can pass judgment. I am assured that chaos reigns in the three hundred and thirty-two languages of India.

There, my dear Father, that explains why I do not like your anaphoras. They have effectively killed the Roman Mass.

I never had an answer from the priest concerned. That is the trouble in answering letters to unknown persons: one simply does not know whether they really want an answer or whether they merely wish to show how intelligent they are. Anyway, I published the above answer because I doubt if sufficient attention has been paid to the disappearance of *the* Mass. The human choice in the "masses of Masses" has totally desacralised the proceedings.

Of course, I sometimes had to answer highly intelligent letters. Both the following letters are to a friend who visited me in Viviers. I had given him a copy of my *Irreligion* [see chapter 16], which had just been published, as he reads French easily. The first letter is dated March 27th, 1988.

❖ ❖ ❖

Dear X.,

Thank you so much for your kind letter. I feel highly flattered that you should have taken my *Irreligion* seriously—but I'm not surprised that you should disagree.

You write: "I suppose that I believe vaguely in a God since, all things being contingent, there must be an incontingent Being somewhere, somehow. But that is as far as I go. I mistrust all historical religions precisely because time (history) is the most contingent thing we know... I suppose I could cast myself as a non-practicing Buddhist, since they allow for the contingent human to be reabsorbed into the incontingent Being... but I totally fail to understand Christianity. There is presumably the historical fact of the crucifixion of a good man, but it is surrounded with evident myths, from the virgin birth to the resurrection... Tell me, Bryan, why you, a convert, really believe in Christianity—as I know you do, utterly and sincerely."

My dear X., I cannot tell you why I believe because I do so with every fibre of my being. It is a fact, as inexplicable as the fact that I am Bryan Houghton. I accept both unquestioningly. The only true answer would be that I believe owing to the grace of God—but you would not allow that. However, I do occasionally get depressed and my faith yearns for a bit of rational buttressing from rational evidence. This, obviously, I can express.

I have a host of buttresses, but there is one which is predominant. Curiously enough, you mention it in your letter: "the historical fact of the crucifixion of a good man."

Now let us start off with your incontingent Being—God. In all other religions or irreligions, the incontingent Being enjoys his omnipotence in the eternal happiness of his infinite perfection. God everlastingly twiddles his thumbs. But he creates contingent beings—ourselves—to whom he distributes misfortune and suffering. Moreover, he expects us to bear suffering nobly, even to the point of martyrdom for his name's sake. Since there is no true nobility other than suffering nobly borne, the human becomes far more noble than God. God is a coward who expects me to do what he is unwilling to do himself.

Therein lies the fundamental revelation of Christianity: God is not a coward; He does not expect others to bear what He is unwilling to bear himself. In fact, He becomes incarnate (hence your "myths" of the virgin birth and resurrection) precisely to do as man what He cannot do as God.

No, my dear X., Christianity is of necessity the only true religion because it alone makes God nobler than man. We have our misfortunes and sufferings to bear but we know that they have all been borne by God.

And do you expect a dozen fisherman from the Lake of Galilee to have invented this shattering view of things which, once invented, cannot be invented twice?...

The second letter to the same friend is nearly three months later. It is dated June 15th, 1988.

Dear X.,

I was most gratified that you should be able to "see the point of a God that suffers."

However, you return to the attack with the Real Presence: "I cannot accept a religion whose principal focus of worship is an unverifiable assumption, clean contrary to all physical evidence. I refer of course to the Real Presence. I am glad to learn that some of your men are now talking about 'symbolic reality' and 'trans-signification' instead of 'trans-substantiation.' Is this what you really mean?"

No, it is not what I mean. I mean "the Real Presence of Jesus Christ, body, blood, soul and divinity, under the appearance of bread and wine."

To "see the point" of the Real Presence one has to return to the suffering God.

He really does suffer, even to the point of death. The crime committed against Him is quite inconceivable: it is deicide, the killing of God incarnate. But what evidence or memorial could He possibly leave of this event? He owned exactly nothing; they had even cast lots for His clothes. He died stark naked. His only property as man was His body and blood. This is precisely what He left.

It is at this point that enters the sublimity of His testament. What He has left is the real, physical evidence of the most inconceivable crime: deicide. And He leaves it as the guarantee of salvation of the criminals.

Can you conceive a more divine Act?

Such is the basis of Catholic belief in the Real Presence.

You will notice that the problem between us is not "rational": we both have our "reasons" for believing or disbelieving. The problem is one concerning the "criterion of truthful." To you the criterion is "what can be *reduced* to a physical analysis." To me, it is "what can be *expanded* to the sublime." To you, all truth is a phenomenon; to me, all truth is God.

How does this come about? We have much the same social background. We are both well educated. I am not ten years your senior. We get on very well together and I look forward to your next visit. Yet I am as deeply religious as you are not.

I think the reason is largely due to our formation. You are a scientist and a distinguished mathematician. I am an humble historian.

Now, the scientific process is one of analysis. You analyse the phenomenon to the umpteenth degree. This analysis gives you "facts," not "truth." From your analysis your mathematics give you diverse "hypotheses" as to how things work—but again, a hypothesis is not a truth. It seems to me that you fall easily into a state of mind in which only facts are true—and one must remain agnostic concerning the hypotheses.

I, as an humble historian, am used to the reverse process. I am constantly trying to find the truth concerning an historical event by synthesising all the known phenomena, including the moral motives of the human participants.

In fact, your formation leads you to "reductionism" by analysis of phenomena. Mine leads me to "expansionism" by a synthesis of phenomena—including human acts, with all their sublimity and turpitude.

Enough!

I only hope that you will "expand" your views to include the whole gamut of human endeavour and experience—the sublime truths as well as the analytical facts—and that you will be able to "see the point" of the Real Presence as you did that of a "suffering God."

Devotedly…

I don't see anything particularly dreadful in the last letter. But the fact remains that I received no answer and the friend concerned has not returned to Viviers. I have noticed, however, that atheists and agnostics are far more sensitive to criticism than are theists. We take criticism for granted; we even doubt and criticise ourselves. I often wonder if the atheist or agnostic has terrible temptations to believe. Does he, tossing in his bed in bitter anguish, ejaculate a prayer: "O god! Help my unbelief! Give me the certainty of your non-existence! Preserve me from the very idea that you are!" If he does, he is at least a human being and has my respect. But, judging by the smooth self-satisfaction of most agnostics whom I know, they never have a temptation in their lives. I prefer religious people: they may be rogues, but some of them are jolly—and they can be saints.

185

20

The Present Situation

Lefebvre excommunicated himself by consecrating four bishops on July 30th, 1988. Has there been any change in the Church since then?

It is really rather pathetic. We, the traditionalists who had always remained loyal to Rome, thought that we should be received back into the fold with fanfares of delight now that Archbishop Lefebvre had strayed irremediably. Not a bit of it! Those who had followed Lefebvre but recanted, such as the admirable Dom Gérard Calvet, got pats on the back from Rome—although less cordial pats from the local bishops. But those who had never followed Lefebvre, such as the members of Una Voce, the Latin Mass Society and myself, got little more than a sneer: "More fools you for not joining Lefebvre!" The fact is that in the eyes of the Church only bishops count. The Lefebvrists have an Archbishop to support them. The extraordinary fact is that Una Voce, the Latin Mass Society and the like have not a single bishop in the world to come to their rescue. There must be well over three thousand bishops in the world, counting diocesan, titular, retired and auxiliary bishops, but not one has thought fit to support publicly Una Voce or the Latin Mass Society. It shows with what care bishops are chosen!

It so happens that I have faculties in two French dioceses, those of Viviers (the right bank of the Rhône south of Lyons) and of Valence (the left back of Rhône south of Lyons). In England I am incardinated (quite illegally) in two dioceses, those of Northampton and of East Anglia.

Let us take France first.

The Bishop of Viviers: As I think I have already said, he is a

charming, intelligent, cultured man; all he lacks is a bit of religion. I like him very much. He has not organised a single Tridentine Mass in the whole of his diocese. The last priest whom I knew
to say one secretly was dear Abbé Duroure, who died recently
(February 1990). I get rumours that there are two other priests in
the north of the diocese who say it—but I have no proof.

The Bishop of Valence: There is the Benedictine priory of Triors near Romans (under the Abbot of Randol). There is an
extreme Lefebvrist somewhere in the valley of the Isère. In the
extreme south of the diocese, Rochegude is served by a monk
from Dom Gérard's monastery. That, as far as I know, is all, for a
large and important diocese. There is nothing at Valence itself.

Mind you, even in France things are changing. As I have said, I
say Sunday Mass in a large private chapel in Montélimar. Of old,
when I came to England I had to close the chapel down because I
could not find a supply priest: the permission to say the old Mass
had been given personally to me and to nobody else. Now I can
nominate a supply, and indeed last year one of the supplies was
the vicar general of the diocese! My sacristan (a retired colonel,
used to bossing people about) had to correct him a few times; but
the Mass was duly said!

In fact, there is the minimum possible change in France.

Exactly the same applies to England.

Firstly, the Diocese of Northampton. Here the late bishop,
Charles Grant, was a personal friend of mine. He was as charming a man as [he was] an incompetent bishop. It will be remembered that he came out to Viviers expressly to simplify my life. In
this diocese I have always been *persona grata* and could say public
Tridentine Masses, notably at Slough, the parish which I
founded. But, as far as I know, there is not a single church or
chapel in which the Tridentine Mass is allowed on a permanent
basis. And the diocese contains a part of Berkshire and all Buck-
inghamshire, Bedfordshire, Huntingdonshire and Northampton-
shire—a large slice of central England, with a number of
industrial towns from Slough in the south, via Luton, Bedford,
Milton-Keynes and Northampton, up to Peterborough in the
north. It is a large chunk to be deprived of the Tridentine Mass.

Incidentally, I was in England when Charles Grant was dying. I

did not call on him as I knew he hated visitors. He preferred to sit
and meditate through dense clouds of tobacco smoke. However,
he heard that I was in the neighbourhood and got somebody to
ring me. I duly turned up and was my usual self. He interrupted
me: "Bryan, I want you to know that I can still just say Mass. I do
not say it in Latin, but I do say it silently. You were right." It was
for that disclosure that he had called me over. Dear Charles! He
died soon after.

The Diocese of East Anglia is more tricky. The bishop is a certain Alan Clark. I liked him and trusted him when he first became
auxiliary to Grant. Twenty-five years later I still like him but trust
him less; he is too involved in ecumenicity. Anyway, he has
allowed the old Mass in a remote village in East Suffolk. I believe
that negotiations are proceeding for a permanent church in Norwich. His vicar general allows me to say a public Mass on Sunday
in my old parish of Bury St Edmunds—once a year! But Bishop
Clark is saddled with two illicit old Massers: Father Oswald
Baker, who was once my curate in Slough and now functions at
Downham Market in Norfolk; Father Silk, with whom I corresponded when he was a high-church Anglican, who got himself
ordained, presumably at Écône, and who now functions in Cambridge. These two slightly egregious priests tend to prejudice
Clark against the traditional Mass.

Both in England and in France the pope's request[1] that the
indult of 1984 should be liberally used is a dead letter. It is a far
cry today from the spirit after the Council when any Roman
permission was hailed with the slogan: "Permissions are given in
order to be used!" Now, apparently, a papal permission is
expressly given so as not to be used.

No, I think that I am being slightly unfair on France. There has
been a hesitant attempt to implement the indult. In Paris, Cardinal Lustiger has given a parish church in central Paris for the use
of traditionalists—their weddings, baptisms, funerals, etc.—apart
from allowing the old Mass in a good number of parishes. Cardinal Decourtray of Lyons is grudgingly following suit. He too has
allowed a (not very central) traditionalist parish. Of the ninety-

1 Motu Proprio *Ecclesia Dei adflicta* (1988), 6c.

seven diocesan bishops in France, seven, to my certain knowledge, are well disposed towards the traditionalists. Two of them are recent appointments and show which way the wind is blowing. But all that is fairly superficial—an attempt at appeasement.

What is important is that four large abbeys of Benedictine monks and two of nuns have opted for the old Mass. They are: (for men) Fontgombault, Randol, Le Barroux and Triors (this is still a priory but will soon be erected into an abbey); (for women) Jouques and Le Barroux. Now, it must be remembered that the *practical totality* of European civilization descends from the two abbeys of Subiaco and Monte Cassino. Great abbeys are rather like atomic plants: although totally cut off from the world, they radiate spirituality and culture. It is true that the abbeys will have episcopal barbarians to contend with, but barbarians they are— and will eventually give way to the process of civilization. I have great trust in abbeys.

But in England the situation is different. Doubtless the Carthusians at Parkminster have returned to their old Mass. But England is full of Benedictines. Has a single monastery returned to the Mass of Saint Benedict? Now, I can hear some monk giggling: "Saint Benedict never said the Tridentine Mass!" Of course not! But there is at least continuity if not identity between the Roman Missal of the late sixteenth century and that of 1962. To my mind, it passes belief that not a single Benedictine community in England has claimed its heritage.

However, I shall die in peace, reasonably certain that the old Mass will return, albeit that I am well aware that it is still not permitted. It is only certain *people* who are *permitted* to say it—but there is no general permission for the old Mass as such at the time of writing in April 1990. This is perfectly scandalous. It is, however, evident that a general permission will come if the number of priests permitted to say it increases.[2]

But that is not the sort of argument which inspires me with confidence. No, the fact is that the new religious outlook has been tailored to suit the world of the 1950s/1960s. Evidently, that

---

2 A prediction fulfilled in the Motu Proprio *Summorum Pontificum* of 2007.

world is crumbling before our eyes. It won't much matter what Mass is said for the five percent of faithful remaining in the West, but it will matter what is said in the ex-communist countries. A catechism will also be needed[3]—and a Catholic translation of the Bible. In fact, the communist countries will need a bit of God-centred (theocentric) religion, exactly what the new outlook has rejected in the West in favour of a man-centered (anthropocentric) religion.

I even have hopes in the West. The honeymoon between science and progress seems to be running into difficulties. Scientists realise that they can do what they should not. They could destroy all life on this earth, but the result would be undesirable. This implies a moral law. But a moral law is the last thing they want. Nevertheless, it pokes up its ugly head. Yes, I have great hopes of the scientists finding their way to God. It would make some of our bishops look as stupid as they are.

Anyway, here I am in 1990, in my eightieth year, writing my memoirs precisely when I am losing my memory. It is an amusing process. I have no regrets in life for the simple reason that all the important events appear utterly inevitable. That I became a Catholic, was ordained a priest, was appointed to Slough and Bury St Edmunds, that I retired to Viviers in France—is all equally inevitable. The only thing which does not appear inevitable is the kindness and loyalty of my friends. I cannot be a very bad man to have made so many.

On March 31st, 1990 I celebrated the fiftieth anniversary of my ordination in the cathedral at Viviers. I preached the following little sermon.

Yes, it is fifty years since my ordination. Five of us were ordained by Cardinal Hinsley in the crypt of Westminster Cathedral for fear of the bombs. We were all late vocations. Only the two youngest have survived: Gordon Wheeler, a good bishop, and myself.

---

3 Fulfilled in the *Catechism of the Catholic Church* of 1994.

Unwanted Priest

After ordination I was nearly fifteen years at Slough, an industrial town to the west of London, where I founded a parish on the Trading Estate. It is here that I learned my trade. Next, just over fifteen years at Bury St Edmunds, then the county town of West Suffolk. But my longest stay has been for over twenty years at Viviers, in exile and without any responsibility.

Generally in life it is our work and responsibilities which give us the necessary discipline to live. But a certain amount of interior discipline is needed to last twenty years with no responsibility and unemployed—thanks to the shameful "exclusiveness" of the new Mass.

But it is precisely the *contemplative* old Mass which has given me that discipline.

You have in front of you a priest rejected because of the old Mass, but whom the old Mass alone keeps going.

BRIAN HOUGHTON, 11th April, 1990.

About the Author

BRYAN HOUGHTON (1911–1992), of Anglican background, was received into the Catholic Church in Paris in 1934 and ordained a priest on March 30, 1940. Throughout the 1960s he found himself increasingly at odds with the self-styled "reformers" who, in the name of Vatican II, were wreaking havoc in the Church. On the day the *Novus Ordo Missae* went into effect—November 30, 1969, the first Sunday of Advent—he resigned from his pastorship at Bury St Edmunds, refusing to celebrate with the new missal. Drawing on his inheritance, he purchased a property with a chapel in the region of Viviers in the south of France and, with his bishop's consent, continued to offer the Tridentine Mass for a small congregation until his death on November 19, 1992. He wrote two novels, *Mitre and Crook* and *Judith's Marriage*, the present collection of essays, *Unwanted Priest*, and a children's book, *Saint Edmund, King and Martyr*.

Made in United States
North Haven, CT
08 November 2022

26430310R00125